MILLENNIUM 2000

RAPTURE OR JUBILEE

by DONALD J. SNEEN

KIRK HOUSE PUBLISHERS
Minneapolis, Minnesota

MILLENNIUM 2000

RAPTURE OR JUBILEE

Library of Congress Cataloging-in-Publication data
Sneen, Donald J.
        Millennium 2000:Rapture of Jubilee / Donald J. Sneen
        p. cm.
        ISBN 1-886513-00-7
        1. Millennium—theology. 2. Church—doctrines. 3. Sects—end times.
I. Title.
                                                    99-96537
                                                    CIP

Kirk House Publishers, PO Box 390759, Minneapolis, MN 55439
Manufactured in the United States of America

CONTENTS

PREFACE

We stand at the threshold of the millennium crossing—the year 2000 as the world regards it. The secular media reminds us of "millennium moments," "millennium milestones," and the technological urgency to be ready for the big changes (Y2K). Actually, the 21st century and the third millennium begin with January 1, 2001!

Strictly speaking, we have already missed the millennium crossing! Although we do not know the exact date of Jesus' birth, both Matthew and Luke tell us that he was born during the reign of Herod the Great, who died in 4 B.C. (Matthew 2:1 and Luke 1:5). So Jesus was at least four years, or more likely six or seven years old in the year 1. We should be in the year 2003 or 2004 or even later!

This curious state of affairs goes back to a sixth century monk's mistake. Pope John I (523-526) asked Dionysius Exiguus (Dennis the Little) to determine the true date of Easter. Eventually Dionysius, an eminent scholar as well as a pious man, produced a 95-year table of Easter dates. But when Dionysius published his tables he made a reform that was little noticed in his day but now affects all of us: the system of dating known as A.D. (Anno Domini, the year of our Lord). Dionysius dropped the Diocletian calendar, which established Year 1 as the date of the Roman Emperor Diocletian's coronation. He preferred a calendar dating from the birth of Jesus. Dionysius calculated, by means unknown today, that Jesus' birth occurred 531 years before the year in which he was living. That became Year A.D. 1 for Dionysius and eventually for the whole world.

CHAPTER 1

(ᗰILLEᑎᑎIAL FEVEᖇ

"For everything there is a season, and a time for every matter under heaven" (Ecclesiastes 3:1). As we cross from one millennium to another, we are more conscious of times and seasons. For some this is merely a milestone; for business people it represents the challenge of Y2K. For others, especially those of a religious persuasion, it is an apocalyptic time. There was great apprehension in western Christendom as the year 1000 approached. Now there are tabloids stating that Christ will return in the year 2000. In this chapter, I will make a brief comparison of the religious and social responses in the closing years of the two millenia.

THE TENTH CENTURY

The tenth century of the Christian era was "the darkest of the dark ages, a century of ignorance and superstition, anarchy and crime in church and state."[1] The demoralization began in the state, spread to the church, and extended to the papacy. The Holy Roman Empire, having reached its zenith with the crowning of Charlemagne in 800, was in disorder and decay. Most of Charlemagne's successors were weak rulers and no match for the challenges facing their lands and people.

Europe was suffering from invasions by hordes of pagan barbarians. In the ninth century, the Vikings came from the north, pillaging monasteries and attacking cities in Britain, Ireland, and France. While these raids became less frequent in the tenth century as the Vikings engaged in colonization efforts, the damaging effects remained, especially on monasteries. In the south, the Saracens from North Africa overran Sicily and southern Italy, turning the land into a wilderness. The Magyars came from the east and, like hordes of wild beasts, invaded Germany and parts of Italy. Only in Spain, with the rule of the Islamic Moors, was there relative peace and order.

In the political arena, corruption and violence were commonplace. Kings, nobles, and barons fought each other, oppressing the common people and dividing the spoils. The popular contempt with which rulers were regarded was expressed in epithets like "the Bald," "the Fat," "the Simple," "the Lazy." Law and order collapsed as robbers roamed the land and went unpunished. Under feudalism, the masses were uneducated, ignorant, unwashed, and impoverished. Monasteries were occasional lights in the darkness, the Cluniac reform being the brightest example of enlightenment.

In the turbulent tenth century the papacy lost all independence and dignity. Pope followed pope, 25 in one century.[2] Greed, immorality, and violence corrupted the Holy See of St. Peter. The early decades of the century became known as the period of papal pornocracy, with a succession of shameless popes and mistresses. In 954, an 18-year-old youth named Octavian (for the ancient Roman Augustus) was elected pope. He retained that name as civil ruler, but as pope took the name John XII. Whether Octavian or John, he was an immoral and wicked man. Finally, at a Synod convened by Emperor Otto the Great, he was charged with monstrous crimes and deposed in 963. Reasonable people were asking: "Is not this man the Antichrist, sitting in the temple of God, and showing himself as God?" With John XII deposed, the papacy for a brief period was morally cleansed, but it lost its independence.

After the death of Emperor Otto in 973, a disgraceful power struggle broke out between imperial popes and anti-popes, culminating in the murder of John XIV in 984. After the sudden and suspicious death of the first German pope, Gregory V (996-999), Gerbert, archbishop of Rheims, was elected pope with the consent of Emperor Otto III. The first French pope, Gerbert, became Sylvester II. An ecclesiast of unusually great learning and integrity, he would usher in the next millennium— if there would be one!

There was a widespread belief in Christendom that there would not be another millennium: *It is written that when a thousand years shall have rolled by, he shall come back to us. At the stroke of the last hour, he shall come back to earth.*

Anticipating the coming judgment, thousands of pilgrims set out eastward for Palestine to greet the Lord at his return. In response to a call for help, Pope Sylvester issued a pastoral letter of support. This letter gave the first papal impulse to the crusades almost a century later in 1096. Of the multitudes who left their families and fields, only a small minority reached Jerusalem. Countless numbers died on the way of hunger, thirst and disease. Others were captured by Saracens, Lombards, and Greeks, and sold into slavery.

In the last year of the old millennium, fields in Europe were left unplowed and unplanted. The second coming of the Lord would not witness Paradise on earth, but the end of the world. The last days of autumn were not spent gathering food and fuel for winter, but with prayers in homes and churches. Amazing miracles were reported, and signs in the skies, including an eclipse, intensified the excitement. Scornful skeptics fell silent. Millennial monks and parish priests preached the coming judgment in powerful language. When the final day came, throngs of people crowded the churches of England, France, Italy, and Germany. Bells throughout Christendom tolled their fateful message: *At the stroke of the last hour he shall come back.* In Rome, Pope Sylvester presided at mass in St. Peter's as the final hour approached. Trembling hands made the sign of the cross over their breasts and in the air and over one another. Each minute seemed an eternity. The midnight hour came, and nothing happened. The world had not ended, and Paradise had not come to earth. "But the first millennium passed, and Christendom awoke with a sigh of relief on the first day of the year 1001."[3]

THE TWENTIETH CENTURY

In writing to the believers at Corinth in the sixth decade of the first century, the apostle Paul recommended the status quo and even celibacy:

"I mean, brothers and sisters, the appointed time has grown short; from now on, let even those who have wives be as though they had none, and those who mourn as though they were not mourning, and those who rejoice as though they were not rejoicing, and those who buy as though they had no possessions, and those who deal with the world as though they had no dealings with it. For the present form ("morphe") of this world is passing away" (I Corinthians 7:29-31).

Paul regarded the end of the age and the second coming of Christ as imminent. Without giving up his belief in the return of Christ, Paul modified his view in the later writings of Philippians and Colossians. The common denominator for Paul in the first century, for many Europeans in the tenth century, and for unknown numbers of people in the late twentieth century is the *attitude* that the present form ("morphe") of this world is passing away. This world is transitory, has a terminal illness, and will not continue long on its present course. Apocalyptic is an attitude and a body of literature. And *events* shape people's attitudes. For Paul and early Christians it was the conviction that the risen and ascended Messiah Jesus would shortly return in glory. In the tenth century, the heathen raids on monasteries and the corruption of kings and popes reinforced the belief that Christ would return at the end of a literal thousand years of Christendom. For us in the twentieth century the population explosion, pollution, world wars, and the nuclear threat are viewed by many as warnings and signs of the end-times in fulfilment of Scripture. I have even heard secularists say that "it is one minute to midnight!"

The very chronology of a thousand years exerts a gravitational pull on human imagination, with fear and faith comingling at the threshold of the millennial crossing. The millennial excitement in Jerusalem, particularly that generated by the Miller cult and occasionally other groups, are examples of this phenomenon. Cults are especially prone to millennial excesses. The predictions of sixteenth century Nostradamus recently sent a non-Christian Japanese cult into frenzied violence. In the western world there have been many religious and several secular cults of an apocalyptic character. The five examples that follow illustrate the common elements of these cults, whether religious or secular. First, the leader, as a divine pretender, claims absolute authority and commands total obedience. Secondly, the world is evil, and salvation is escape from this hostile planet. Finally, in obeying the leader, the desire to escape becomes self-fulfilling and ends in disaster and death.

Jonestown

In a November 1978 Sunday issue of *The New York Times* a banner headline stated: "Guyana toll is raised to at least 900, with 260 children among the victims." Behind this bizarre tragedy in an isolated South American encampment was a charismatic Protestant minister from San Francisco, Rev. Jim Jones.

Born in Indiana, Jones had moved to San Francisco in the early 1960s. There he organized a congregation, People's Temple, and developed community service projects, including child care and a kitchen to feed the poor. He was also involved in political campaigns, and his work received endorsements from local and even national leaders.

The membership of People's Temple never exceeded 2500, but Jones spoke to a much larger audience at rallies and healing services. His message was an eclectic mix of communist and even anarchic ideas delivered with the style of a fundamentalist preacher. The theme of *apocalyptic doom* was an early part of his message, having its origins in Jones' fear of nuclear annihilation. His ideas became increasingly wild, with Jones claiming at various times to be the incarnation of Jesus Christ, Ikhnaton, Buddha, Lenin, and Father Divine.

By 1974, in cooperation with the government of Guyana, Jones was making plans for a religious community in the remote interior of that South American country. He and hundreds of followers made the move in 1977. In this secluded community Jones exercised *complete control* over the members. Defections or threats of defections from this paradise made him increasingly paranoid. Matters hit the fan in November 1978. Acting on reports of mistreatment of members and an arms build-up, Congressman Leo Ryan from San Francisco, together with several journalists and relatives of Temple members, made a fact-finding trip to Guyana. After meeting with Jones at the colony, Ryan's group was joined by four cult members who had chosen to defect. As they were about to board the plane at the nearby landing strip, Ryan and several others were shot and killed. Hearing of the murders, Jones told his followers that they would soon be attacked by the CIA and that they should prepare for a revolutionary death. Fruit punch laced with cyanide was prepared; babies and children were forced to drink the potion, followed by adults. The final toll, which included Jones, was 914 dead, of whom 216 were children.

Jonestown Revisited?

The Branch Davidian tragedy of April 1993 recalled memories of Jonestown 1978. The Branch Davidians of Waco, Texas, was a communal group under the control of one Vernon Howell, who had emerged as cult leader following a power struggle with the son of the community's founder.

A charismatic speaker who was immersed in the book of Revelation, Howell changed his name to David Koresh (after Cyrus the Great?) and *claimed to be the Messiah*. As such he declared himself "worthy to open the book" and interpret its seals concerning the events of the last days (cf. Revelation 5:2). Armed with this claim, Koresh took *absolute control* of the community. At his command, men even turned over their wives to Koresh to that he might populate the world with his "seed."

Fearing outside intervention, the Branch Davidians amassed a supply of heavy weapons. From their apocalyptic perspective, this was a defense against Satanic government forces. The arms build up brought the federal government into the drama. When Treasury agents moved to disarm the Davidians on February 28, four federal agents were shot and killed. A siege followed, with government authorities vainly trying to negotiate a surrender. But rational discussion proved fruitless. Finally, concerned especially for the welfare of the 17 children in the compound, Attorney General Janet Reno authorized a tank attack on April 19. Branch Davidian members set fire to their structure, and it burned to the ground with all 86 members perishing in the inferno. An apocalyptic psychopath, Koresh was willing to take himself and his followers to a fiery finish since he believed that he would be resurrected and revealed to the world as a risen messiah.

Heaven's Gate

As a pluralistic society, the United States has been a greenhouse for many neo-religious movements, Christian and non-Christian. Some eventually disappear, usually after their leader dies. Others, like the Moonies, move toward integration into the mainstream of religious life.

Heaven's Gate should be characterized as a secular apocalyptic cult, with a mixture of New Age thought, apocalyptic ideas, and science fiction space travel. It was a separatist group, isolated and mobile, and this was probably responsible for its doom.

Many of the Heaven's Gate members were well-educated professional people who regarded a man called DO as their personal representative. DO was one of the names used by Marshall Herff Applewhite, a former opera singer who became the leader of the cult and died with the members.

A key idea was "separation from the world." The following appeared on the Heaven's Gate web site: "Unless you are currently an active student or are attempting to become a student of the present Representative from the Kingdom of Heaven—you ARE STILL 'of the world,' having done no significant separation from worldliness, and you are still serving the opposition to the Kingdom of Heaven."

This was signed by DO, "The Present Representative."

The unpredicted appearance of the comet Hale-Bopp stirred apocalyptic excitement among the Heaven's Gate members. In their gnostic and pseudo-scientific view, they believed that a UFO trailing the comet would transport them to a "Level Above Human." This led to the suicide in California of 39 members on March 27, 1997.

The Jouret Cult

In October 1994, Swiss police, investigating reports of a ritualized mass suicide, found the bodies of 23 men, women, and children at a farm in Cheiry, and 25 more bodies in a mountain hamlet about 100 miles north of Cheiry. At the same time as these discoveries, there was a fatal fire north of Montreal, Canada that claimed four lives.

All of the 52 victims were part of a cult headed by Luc Jouret, a 46-year-old Canadian-Belgian. News accounts in Switzerland and Canada reported that the group held to New Age ideas and embraced literal apocalyptic views that led them to stockpile weapons in preparation for the end of the world. In 1993, when Canadian authorities issued a warrant for Jouret's arrest, he fled to Switzerland. An ex-wife of a cult member testified that "Jouret pretended to be Christ," warning people of a coming catastrophe in which only the chosen would survive." [4]

Millennium Mania in Jerusalem

Officials in Israel fear that the end of the millennium will bring more threats to that nation's security from apocalyptic sects. Early in January 1999, an American cult group from Denver, led by Kim Miller, was rounded up and deported from Israel. In December the disappearance of Miller and his followers, who called themselves "Concerned Christians," had raised concerns among relatives and neighbors. Israeli authorities feared the group might commit mass suicide or instigate a suicidal shootout with police on the Temple Mount.

Like Jim Jones, Miller was once a respected religious leader. He had been engaged in a counter-cult ministry and spoke in some of Denver's largest churches. Then he turned against the organized churches, accusing them of teaching New Age and Satanic ideas. In recent years Miller declared himself to be the last prophet on earth and claimed that he could channel the voice of God. In December 1998, he predicted that he would die in the streets of Jerusalem and be resurrected three days later.

Miller's actions were not the first of this kind in Jerusalem, nor are they likely to be the last. A number of pilgrims gripped by messianic mania have put on white garb and identified themselves with biblical figures, like Elijah or Jesus. They shout and call attention to themselves. While such behavior may only be a nuisance, it has occasionally taken a far more serious turn. In 1969, an Australian Christian fundamentalist, Dennis Rohan, set fire to the Al Aqsa Mosque on the Temple Mount. This touched off riots by Moslems in Israel and as far away as India in which many people died.

Dr. Yair Bar-El of the Israeli Psychiatric Society predicts that some 40,000 of the four million tourists expected in Israel in years 1999 and 2000 will require psychiatric help as a result of messianic mania, or "Jerusalem Syndrome." He estimates that about 800 will require temporary hospitalization. These people will be expecting apocalyptic events like the battle of Gog and Magog, the raising of the dead and the return of Jesus Christ.

The millennial threats are being taken seriously by Israel's security and intelligence forces. Even the Mossad, which ordinarily deals only with espionage cases, is involved. With the approach of the year 2000, Israel has announced a $12 million security plan to prevent "millennium fanatics" from attacking holy sites in Jerusalem. There are reports that a Christian sect plans to destroy Moslem shrines on the Temple Mount to hasten the rebuilding of the Jewish Temple and prepare the way for Christ's second coming. Israeli police have recently installed sophisticated security devices on all approaches to the Temple Mount and assigned a special force of 400 men to guard the holy site around the clock.[5]

CHAPTER 2

CHRISCIAN MILLENNIALISM

One of the most difficult sections for biblical interpretation is that of the thousand year reign of Christ in Revelation 20. The only actual mention of the millennium in the Bible occurs in this chapter. With the judgment upon the oppressors of God's people completed, all is now ready for the vision of the final triumph of Christ. The martyrs are raised to reign with Christ for a thousand years. In the history of biblical interpretation, this theme has been understood in a variety of ways. In general, these fall into three schools of interpretation: premillennial, amillennial, and postmillennial.

PREMILLENNIAL

In the history of Christian thought, the premillennial view is the oldest school of interpretation. For the first three centuries of the Christian era, the millennium was envisioned as a future period when Christ and his saints would visibly reign on earth for a literal thousand years. This was the teaching of great theologians like Papias, Irenaeus, Justin Martyr, Tertullian, Hippolytus, Methodius, and others. The notable exception was Origen, who interpreted the thousand years allegorically instead of literally.

The premillennial interpretation is derived from a literal reading of New Testament sections, especially Revelation 19-20. At his second coming Christ and his heavenly armies will conquer and destroy the Antichrist and his forces (Rev. 19:17-21). Satan will be bound and thrown into the bottomless pit for a thousand years (Rev. 20:1-3). During this millennium Christ and the martyred saints, who have been resurrected, will visibly reign on earth (Rev. 20:4-5). At the end of the thousand years, Satan will be released and come out to deceive the nations and lead them in a rebellion against God. The final war occurs with the devil defeated and thrown into the lake of fire. This is followed by a second resurrection in which all those raised are brought before the throne of God to be judged according to their deeds. Death and Hades are thrown into the lake of fire, which is the second death. The final victory over the hostile forces of the Antichrist, Satan, and Death is followed by the vision of the new heaven and new earth, in which God dwells with humankind in a renewed creation (Rev. 21:1ff.).

There were similar Jewish views regarding the Messiah's reign on earth. I Enoch 1-36 and the Testament of the Twelve Patriarchs, which were pre-Christian, tell of a thousand year future Messianic rule. The rabbi Eliezer ben Hyrcanus, writing about A.D. 90, suggested a thousand year Messianic period. At approximately the same time, the writer of II Esdras believed that the Messiah would rule for 400 years (7:28-30). At the end of these years "my son, the Messiah" shall die, along with all other human beings. The world would then return to primeval silence for seven days followed by a general judgment, the resurrection of the good and the wicked, and the final end.

The evidence suggests that the premillennial concept of a Messianic reign of a thousand years is of Jewish origin, employing a literal interpretation of biblical texts.

AMILLENNIAL

In explaining and defending this view, Anthony A. Hoekema suggested that the expression "realized millennialism" is a more accurate description of the concept than "amillennialism."[1]   Proponents of this view believe that the millennium of Revelation 20 is not exclusively future but is already now being realized. Hoekema regards "Revelation 20:1-6 as describing what takes place during the entire history of the church, beginning with the first coming of Christ."[2]

Early in the fifth century, St. Augustine interpreted the thousand years allegorically rather than literally. He regarded it as the spiritual reign of Christ in history through the Christian church. For those whom Christ rules Satan is bound. The struggle is not over, but the final victory of Christ over evil is assured. Augustine's eschatology was affirmed in the church's Council of Ephesus in 431. The amillennial intepretation became and continues to be the doctrine of the Roman Catholic church. The reformers, Martin Luther and John Calvin, also accepted Augustine's interpretation, and Lutheran and Calvinist confessional statements affirm this position. Article XVII of *The Augsburg Confession* affirms the return of Christ to raise up the dead and judge all people, but goes on to state:

> Rejected, too, are certain Jewish opinions which are even now making an appearance and which teach that, before the resurrection of the dead, saints and godly men will possess a worldly kingdom and annihilate all the godless.

In summary, amillennialists regard the reign of Christ as already present in the world through the preaching of the Gospel and the saving work of the Holy Spirit in the church. There is a "now" but "not yet" character to Christ's reign; there is a sense in which the world is getting better but another in which the age is getting worse. However, this tension will be overcome when Christ returns in the future, raises the dead, executes judgment, and ushers in the final reign.

POSTMILLENNIAL

In the history of Christian interpretation postmillennialism is of more recent origin. Rejecting a future interpretation of the thousand years, it regards the kingdom of Christ as already present through the preaching of the Gospel and the work of the Holy Spirit in individuals and institutions. It owes much of its thought and dynamic to Daniel Whitby (1638-1726). Whitby believed that the world would be converted to Christ, the Jews restored to their land, and pope and Turks defeated, and the world would eventually enjoy a period of universal peace and righteousness for a thousand years. At the close of this period Christ would return for the last judgment.[3]

In an explanation of this school of interpretation, Loraine Boettner writes:

> The millennium to which the postmillennialist looks forward is thus a golden age of spiritual

prosperity during this present dispensation, that is, during the Church Age. This is to be brought about through forces now active in the world. It is to last an indefinitely long period of time, perhaps much longer than a literal one thousand years. The changed character of individuals will be reflected in an uplifted social, economic, political, and cultural life of mankind. The world at large will then enjoy a state of righteousness which up until now has been seen only in relatively small and isolated groups: for example, some family circles, and some local church groups and kindred organizations."[4]

This does not mean that all sin and evil in the world is abolished, but that evil is "reduced to negligible proportions, that Christian principles will be the rule, not the exception, and that Christ will return to a truly Christianized world."[5]

The redemption of the world is a long and slow process extending over centuries, yet surely approaching its appointed goal, advancing even though there are apparent setbacks. Boettner cites the growth of Christianity in the world through evangelization and mission work as well as social changes, such as the virtual disappearance of slavery and polygamy, as evidence for this optimism. True postmillennialism is not humanistic and evolutionary, as certain critics have charged, but "supernaturalistic through and through."[6]

The response of George Eldon Ladd to the postmillennial discussion is noteworthy. "The argument that the world is getting better is a two-edged sword. One can equally well argue from empirical observation that the world is getting worse."[7] Human presuppositions select the evidence and shape the conclusions.

DISPENSATIONAL PREMILLENNIAL

Dispensational premillennialism, also known as "Darbyism," is a recent development in the long history of Christian interpretation of the end times. Though there are variations within this school, the basic ideas and structure are those of John Nelson Darby.

Dispensational premillennialism shares several elements with classic premillennialism: a literal interpretation of the thousand year reign of Christ on earth, teachings on the Antichrist and the seven year tribulation period, and the final battle of Armageddon.

However, the differences from premillennialism are significant, and over the years there has not been much creative dialogue between the two schools.

Darby taught that God dealt with humankind in a series of epochs or dispensations, with somewhat differing means of salvation in each one. We are now in the dispensation of the Christian Church, that period from Pentecost to the "rapture," when true believers will be caught up to heaven.

Secondly, this school makes a sharp separation between Israel and the Church in God's redemptive plan. Old Testament prophecies about Israel are always interpreted literally with no allowance for a spiritual understanding of the Church as Zion or the New Testament Israel.

Thirdly, Darby's dispensationalism gives Israel a special end-time role. While a few Christians had previously entertained and even encouraged ideas of a Jewish return to Palestine, Darby placed such an event at the center of his system. Dispensationalists now offer virtually unqualified support for the modern country of Israel for theological as well as political reasons.

In general, Darby constructed a tight system of belief, reinforced by numerous biblical proof texts. This methodology continues to be a characteristic of modern dispensationalists.

CHAPTER 3

RAPPING ON THE RAPTURE

You may have seen a bumper sticker sign that reads: "When the rapture comes, this car will not have a driver." The person who attached that sticker is probably dead serious. In this chapter, I will discuss the origins of the rapture idea within the context of its premillennial dispensational theology, and also examine and respond to the presuppositions and methods of this school of thought.

THE ORIGINS OF DISPENSATIONALISM

While prophecy preachers have appeared through the centuries, the dispensational school is of relatively recent origin. In the twelfth century a Cistercian monk, Joachim of Fiore, announced the imminent arrival of a new age. According to him, there are three ages in history, each revealing one of the persons of the Trinity. The first was the age of the Father, characterized by the Law and by fear. The second, from the time of Christ up to 1260, was the Gospel age of grace and faith. The third and final age would be that of the Holy Spirit, characterized by love and spirit.

In the thirteenth and fourteenth centuries certain Franciscan monks believed that they were living in the third age with St. Francis as their messianic leader. They believed in a classless society and rejected the clergy hierarchy, even the pope. In the sixteenth century, Thomas Muentzer, who had been a follower of Luther, became an apocalyptic utopian and worked to set up the kingdom of God in Muenster, Germany. The movement became increasingly wild and ended with Muentzer's violent death.

Timetables from Scripture have been favorite subjects for prophecy preachers. In the United States, William Miller (1792-

1849), a farmer and a Baptist preacher, made extensive studies of the book of Daniel. He reached the conclusion that Christ's second coming would occur "about the year 1843." When nothing happened that year, his followers in New York state set an exact date, October 22, 1844. Many Millerites did not plant crops that spring. There was increasing excitement as October 22 approached, followed by profound disappointment when the Lord did not appear. Miller died a disappointed man. Though the Millerite movement faded, the Seventh Day Adventist denomination originated from it. Some years later Charles Taze Russell, again using calculations from Scripture, predicted that the great judgment would come in 1914. His followers, the Russellites, embarrassed by Russell's cheating people on wheat sales, later changed their name to Jehovah's Witnesses.

After many failed attempts to set a date for the final judgment, they currently say that "millions now living will never die."

There was also a great deal of millennial excitement in Great Britain in the early nineteenth century. In the 1820s a charismatic preacher, Edward Irving, proclaimed Christ's imminent return to earth. His disciples included Henry Drummond, a wealthy banker and a member of Parliament, who organized and funded prophecy conferences. Through these conferences, Drummond and the Irvingites spread their millennial ideas in Great Britain and later in the United States.

The main architect of the premillennial dispensationalist system was an Irish man, John Nelson Darby (1800-1882), who had been influenced by Irving. After studying law and theology, he was ordained by the Church of Ireland (Anglican). He soon became disillusioned with the Anglican church, and joined a new sect, the Brethren, which became the Plymouth Brethren. In the years that followed, Darby travelled extensively in Great Britain and the United States, zealously promoting his beliefs through preaching and prophecy conferences. Having broken with the established church, Darby relentlessly criticized it as a dead church that was "in ruins." He built this into his system, especially with reference to the "apostate church" that would be left on earth at the rapture.

Darby's dispensational ideas reached millions through the work of Cyrus I. Scofield (1843-1921). A veteran of the Confederate army, he became a lawyer in Kansas. After several years of married life he left his wife and two children amidst accusations of taking campaign funds. Jailed in St. Louis on forgery charges, he was converted while in prison by a Darbyite dispensationalist. Upon his release he became a minister. In 1883, while serving as a pastor in Dallas, his wife filed for divorce on grounds of desertion.

Following the Dallas experience, Scofield devoted his time to speaking tours and Bible research and writing. His legacy is the *Scofield Reference Bible* which came out in 1909. Interest in Christ's second coming rose during World War I and sales of the Scofield Bible soared. Millions of copies were sold between 1909 and 1967, when Oxford University Press issued the *New Scofield Reference Bible*. The new issue had sold 2.5 million copies by 1990. Scofield's Bible became the major conduit of premillennial dispensationalism. Scofield combined his notes and the biblical text on the same page and for many readers the notes took on as much authority as the text itself. Though Scofield had relatively little formal education he believed, like William Miller, that any zealous believer could interpret the Bible. He was a gifted writer and confidently explained obscure texts, giving Darby's dispensational system a remarkable unity.

Darby developed a *dispensation* as a span of time in which there was a revelation of God and a test of humanity's obedience to that revelatory act. According to Darby, there are in all of history seven dispensations.[1]

1. **Innocence** (Genesis 1:28-3:13). Here human obedience is tested, resulting in expulsion from the Garden of Eden.

2. **Conscience** (Genesis 3:22-7:23). Having acquired conscience through the first test, God now required humans to use it. They did not measure up (Genesis 6:5) and the dispensation ended with the flood.

3. **Human government** (Genesis 8:20-11:9). Human beings were given the task of governing themselves: Jewish and

Gentile. The Jewish failure ended in their captivities by foreign powers; the Gentile failure ends with the fulfilment of Daniel's prophecy (chapter 2) and judgment of the nations (Matthew 25:31-46).

4. **Promise** (Genesis 12:1; Exodus 19:8). This concerns only Israel, Abraham and his offspring. They are blessed as long as they remain in the promised land. The dispensation ended with Israel foolishly accepting the Law (Exodus 19:8) and giving up God's grace for Law (Exodus 20).

5. **Law** (Exodus 19:8; Matthew 27:35). This dispensation carried on through the balance of the Old Testament and right up to the cross. Israel was tested by the Mosaic law in this long period and failed to measure up to its demands. The test ended with the captivities, but the dispensation continued to Jesus' crucifixion.

6. **Grace** (Romans 3:24; II Timothy 3:1). This began with the Lord's resurrection. God's test is the human response in accepting Jesus Christ as Savior. It will end with the visible Church apostasizing from the faith and God's judgment on it.

7. **Fulness of time** (Ephesians 1:10). This begins with Christ's Second Advent and continues through the millennium. The Kingdom dispensation fulfils the promise to David and his seed regarding the eternal nature of his rule. All previous ages and promises are fulfilled in this seventh dispensation.

The division of the dispensations is arbitrary and puzzling, reflecting Darby's biased views in several areas. Is God's primary relation to humanity that of Judge? Or is God primarily that of Savior? Is not the context for the covenant and Mosaic law God's mighty acts of delivering Israel from slavery (Exodus 19:3-6)? That is Gospel! Is the visible church to be regarded as totally apostate and under God's judgment? Of course there are tares among the wheat, but *God*, not human beings, will separate the wheat from the tares in the final harvest.

The anti-church bias is also evident in the *Scofield Reference Bible.* For example, the church at Thyatira (Revelation 2:18-29) is identified with the papacy; the church at Sardis (Revelation 3:1-6) with the Protestant Reformation. Darby's and Scofield's judgmental attitudes lead to divisions and dissensions among believers, and contradict Paul's exhortation to dwell together in unity within the body of Christ (I Corinthians 1—4).

DISPENSATIONAL CHRONOLOGY OF FINAL EVENTS

This is a general outline of final events according to the dispensationalist system. However, dispensationalists do not totally agree on all details: Darby and Scofield are pre-tribulationist dispensationalists, but others are post-tribulationists, and there are even mid-tribulationist dispensationalists. The pre-tribulationist is the majority point of view and is summarized here; the outline is presented with reference to Revelation 19—20 as their primary source of final events. (It should be noted that in dispensationalist teaching Revelation 4:1-18:24 involves the church or saints that have been raptured and are in heaven, according to their interpretation of Revelation 4:1 and I Corinthians 15:51,52.).

My critical response follows each statement and its description.

1. **The descent of Christ in his millennial character** (Revelation 19:11-21, and 20:2 according to Scofield). This is the return of Christ with his heavenly saints to battle with the beast and false prophet.

Scofield's literary division is puzzling. Revelation 19 is a continuation of the drama in chapter 18; together they form a unit that describes and celebrates Babylon's (Rome) demise. The vision in Revelation 20:1-6 begins a new unit.

When one reads the text there is no reference to a descent of Christ from heaven. (There is an angel that comes down from heaven in 20:1.) The rider on the white horse, who is called Faithful and True and the Word of God, is Christ.

2. **Jesus binds Satan for a thousand years.** A new vision (20:1 ff.) begins with the angel coming down from heaven, having the key to the bottomless pit and a great chain.

The text states that *it is the angel* that seizes and binds Satan and then throws him into the pit (abyss). (There is also reference to binding in Tob 8:3 and the *Testament of Levi* 18:12 (cf. Isaiah 24:22-23; Mark 3:27; Luke 11:14-22).

3. **The thousand year earthly reign of Christ.** This will be a literal thousand years with Jesus ruling along with the martyrs and the nation of Israel from the throne of David in Jerusalem. According to Darby, martyrs who have been in heaven (Revelation 5:6-7; 6:9-11) are now brought down to earth to reign with Christ.

There is no mention of Jerusalem or Israel or an earthly reign in the text (Revelation 20:1-6). (The dispensationalist argument for a political Israel is discussed in the section, "Israel And The Church.")

4. **The loosing of Satan** (Revelation 20:7). The loosing of Satan sets the stage for what follows in the text: Satan's deceiving the nations, Gog and Magog.

In the late first century situation of the church, the loosing of Satan suggests that God's people were being persecuted.

5. **The final battle in history (Armageddon?).** This is the final apostasy at the end of the thousand years. Satan makes his final appeal to unconverted elements in the world. Gog and Magog appeared in Ezekiel 38-39 as persecutors of Israel in the Babylonian captivity. Now they emerge again preparing to battle the saints. Hal Lindsey associated Russia and Red China with Gog and Magog attacking Israel in the final battle at Armageddon (Revelation 16:16).

When the text (20:8-10) is read carefully, Satan is deceiving earthly nations which threaten the saints and holy city; but there is no actual war. There is divine action (holy war?) that saves the saints and the city.

6. **The second resurrection and the final judgment** (Revelation 20:11-15). This is the resurrection of the impenitent dead who are brought before the great white throne. The tribulation

saints and all who belong to Christ were raised in the first resurrection (I Thessalonians 4:14-18; I Corinthians 15:22, 23).

The text states that the dead who are raised are judged for what they have done (cf. Matthew 16:27; Romans 2:6). All people, great and small, are judged—suggesting that they are responsible and accountable. There is no double resurrection. Death and Hades, and those not written in the book of life, are thrown into the lake of fire. This is the second death.

In summarizing Revelation 19—20, there is no descent of Christ from heaven; an angel binds Satan; there is no earthly reign of Christ in Jerusalem; Satan is loosed (persecuting the saints?) to deceive the nations; there is no actual battle of Armageddon but fire from heaven (holy war?) saves the saints and holy city; the dead are raised and judged and Death and Hades are destroyed in the lake of fire, the second death. There is no mention of a rapture or of Jesus coming two times. Most of Darby's system of the end-times, rooted in Revelation 19 and 20, is not found there but is read into the text from his own presuppositions.

THE RAPTURE

The apostle Paul's letters to the church at Thessalonica were written about A.D. 50. They precede the Gospel of Mark by 15 to 20 years and are the first writings in the New Testament. Paul is a contextual writer; most of his letters are responses to problems and issues with which a church was wrestling. In Thessalonica the assembly of believers, so recently converted to Christianity, faced a variety of problems. There was persecution of Christians by the members of the synagogue (2:14-16); and there was the immoral environment of the pagan world. As recent converts from a heathen past, Paul exhorted them to lead moral Spirit-filled lives (4:1-8).

The most urgent problem, however, concerned eschatology. In his mission among them Paul had proclaimed the good news of Jesus' death and resurrection as well as the Lord's second coming. The latter was especially perplexing. In anticipation of the Lord's imminent return, some apparently had quit working and consequently were dependent on other believers. In response, Paul urged them to live quietly and to work with their own hands and be dependent on nobody (4:9-12). Two related questions troubled the congregation. Will Christians who died before Christ's return be saved? And *when* will the Lord return? Paul deals with the first question in 4:13-18, and with the second in 5:1-11.

> But we do not want you to be uninformed, brothers and sisters, about those who have died, so that you may not grieve as others do who have no hope. For since we believe that Jesus died and rose again, even so, through Jesus, God will bring with him those who have died. For this we declare to you by the word of the Lord, that we who are alive, who are left until the coming of the Lord, will by no means precede those who have died. For the Lord himself, with a cry of command, with the archangel's call and with the sound of God's trumpet, will descend from heaven, and the dead in Christ will rise first.
>
> Then we who are alive, who are left, will be caught up in the clouds together with them to meet the Lord in the air; and so we will be with the Lord forever. Therefore encourage one another with these words" (I Thessalonians 4:13-18).

Paul responds to the grief of those who are mourning the death of loved ones, "those who are asleep." The verb for "sleep" (*koimao*, the word "cemetery" is a derivative) in the present tense was a common metaphor among Jews and Greeks for death. However, in contrast to the pagan world, Christians have hope. Therefore, they should not sorrow as unbelievers do. The basis for this hope is Jesus, who "died and rose again." And those believers who have died will be brought back to appear with Jesus when he returns. With confident authority, coming from his call as an apostle, Paul assures the living believers that they have no advantage over those who have died, for these loved ones are already *with the Lord.*

At his coming (*parousia*) Christ will bring these departed believers with him, and the living will be snatched up in the clouds to meet the Lord in the air. The imagery is dramatic and the language is powerful: descent from heaven, archangel's call, the trumpet blast, caught up in the clouds etc. This makes even the most dazzling opening or closing show in the Olympics look puny. Taken literally, the sound should wake the dead and blow the minds of the living. Herein is a cosmic power drama that gathers all of Christ's people, those who have died and those still alive, together with the Lord.

Trying to sort out and specifically analyse each apocalyptic piece of furniture would be speculative. However, the message is about *power* and *who* controls it.

Writing at this time Paul expected the Lord's coming (*parousia*) to be imminent and that he would be alive to experience it. In later writings, he discusses the parousia from another perspective, most powerfully with regard to the resurrection and the nature of the resurrection body. And in the letter to the Philippians, some eight years after the Thessalonian letters, he expected to die before the Lord's return.

I Thessalonians 4:17 is the one specific reference to the rapture in the New Testament. The verb "caught up" (*harpazo*) suggests a violent snatching away of the believers.* Interpreted literally, it becomes the basis for the dramatic and fanciful dramas and scenarios that dispensationalists have spun. How should we understand and interpret this verse?

---

*The verb "*harpazo*" (Latin, "*rapere*") appears several other places in the New Testament. The Roman soldiers "snatched" Paul away from rioters in the Jerusalem council chamber (Acts 23:10); the male child in the vision is "caught up" to save him from the great dragon (Rev. 12:5); Philip is "snatched away" by the Spirit after his meeting with the Ethiopian eunuch (Acts 8:39); after feeding the 5000 in the wilderness, the crowd pursues Jesus to "take him by force" to make him king (John 6:15). Most interesting is Paul's personal vision account that he was "'caught up' to the third heaven—"whether in the body or out of the body I do not know, God knows. And I know that this man was 'caught up' into Paradise . . ." (II Corinthians 12:2,3). See also Matthew 11:12, 12:19, and the noun derivatives in Matthew 23:25, Luke 11:39, and the christological hymn in Philippians 2:6.

Research of ancient customs has shed light on this fascinating section. It is based on a Hellenistic custom of formally receiving a visiting dignitary. The word translated "to meet" (apantesis) in I Thessalonians 4:17 is a technical term in the ancient Greek world to describe a public welcome given by the city to a visiting dignitary. A twentieth century scholar, quoting a number of passages from ancient Greek papyri, inscriptions, and literature, has demonstrated that this was an ancient practice with which Paul and the Thessalonians would have been quite familiar.[2]

In Paul's time, when a city was expecting a visit from royalty or a dignitary, the citizens would go out and stand on either side of the road leading into the city to conduct a formal reception. At the dignitary's arrival the people would welcome him excitedly with loud shouting, blowing trumpets, singing songs, etc. The city officials would usually present an expensive gift to the visitor, who would then lead all the people in a procession back into the city. Once inside the city gates he would usually offer a sacrifice on one or more altars and sometimes pronounce judgment on prisoners, freeing some and sentencing others to death.

Paul, having grown up in the Gentile city of Tarsus, presupposes knowledge of this custom when announcing the second coming in I Thessalonians 4:15-17. But instead of Christians lining the road, he portrays them greeting the Lord in the air. When Christ returns at the end of the age for the great judgment, he is met en route by his followers. The resurrected bodies of the dead and the transformed bodies of the living are "caught up" (*harpazo*) from earth to meet their heavenly king for a glorious reception. But Christ's destination in this journey is earth, not heaven. So he leads his citizens in triumphant procession down to the earth where he will proceed with the final judgment. So instead of a secret "rapture," this event openly signals the end of the present age and the ushering in of the eternal age to come.

Paul concludes this powerful pericope with a promise: "and so we shall always be *with the Lord.*" This promise is the basis for the exhortation: "Therefore comfort one another with these words" (4:18, RSV). Having soared into apocalyptic heights, Paul comes back to earth with a pastoral application to encourage and comfort the anxious and grieving saints in Thessalonica.

Paul wrote I Thessalonians from Corinth, and sent the letter to Thessalonica with his spiritual son and companion Timothy. In a few weeks Timothy returned with troublesome news. The letter had not quieted the eschatological excitement, but it had even gotten worse. Some of the believers thought that the day of the Lord had already come, and they had missed it (II Thessalonians 2:1-2). In his second letter, Paul reminds them of the tradition concerning the day of the Lord. He declares that the rebellion or apostasy must first take place and the "man of lawlessness" be revealed (2:3-10). This evil imposter, who proclaims himself to be God, is now being restrained (2:6-7). Paul does not specify who the "man of lawlessness" (or "man of sin") is or who the "restrainer" is. Some have identified the former with the Antichrist (though Paul never uses the term) and the latter with the Roman empire. There have been other suggestions. Pondering this mysterious passage, St. Augustine admitted that he did not know, but that Paul and the Thessalonians knew who these figures were.

Dispensationalists have cited at least two other texts as evidence for the rapture, I Corinthians 15:51 and Revelation 4:1. There is no mention of a rapture in either passage. Paul discusses the nature of the resurrection body in I Corinthians 15:35-50. His point is that while there are many kinds of bodies, the resurrection body will be an imperishable and spiritual body; the mortal body of "flesh and blood" cannot inherit the kingdom of God. Then he announces a "mystery. . . we shall all be 'changed' in a moment, in the twinkling of an eye, at the last trumpet" (15:51-52). The future verb "we shall be changed" (*allegosemetha*) means "transformed." In some mysterious way, the bodies of believers will be transformed into spiritual bodies in the resurrection.

Dispensationalists argue that after the letters to the seven churches in Revelation 2—3, the church of true believers will be raptured to heaven (Revelation 4:1). They base this on the fact that the word "church" does not occur again in Revelation until 22:16. This is a most interesting argument from silence. But it is hardly strong and convincing! Revelation 4:1-5:14 is the vision of the glory of God and the Lamb, in which the 24 elders and the four living creatures worship around the throne of God. The four living creatures represent all creation. The 24 elders are the twelve patriarchs of the Old Testament and the twelve apostles of the New Testament. Contrary to dispensationalist theology, *both* Israel and the church are participating in the worship. In the end there is no division of the people of God.

ISRAEL AND THE CHURCH

Why are premillennial Christians, and dispensationalists in particular, such strong supporters of the modern country of Israel? The close relationship between the two might seem perplexing to outsiders, but for dispensationalists modern Israel is at the center of their theological system.

For dispensationalists, the Old Testament provides the key for interpreting the New Testament. The Old Testament prophecies concerning Israel are interpreted literally and not figuratively. In the New Testament, concepts like Zion, Jerusalem, the seed of Abraham, and Israel may have a symbolic meaning that refers to the Christian church. Not so, say the dispensationalists. Israel means Israel! It does not mean and cannot mean the church! All the promises and prophecies concerning Israel are earthly and to be understood literally. "The covenants and destinies of Israel are all earthly; the covenants and destinies of the church are all heavenly."[3] This means that the covenants and promises are to be fulfilled to an earthly people upon this earth. To speak of the Christian church as Zion, or of Gentile believers as children of Abraham, is to spiritualize these concepts in an unscriptural manner.

Israel and the church then are distinct and will be separate in the next age. When the Jews rejected Messiah Jesus, God rejected them and chose the church for divine blessings. This is known as "replacement theology." The sixth dispensation of grace is the "Church Age." This is the "Great Parenthesis" between the fifth and seventh dispensation, which will begin with the "rapture." Once the prophetic clock starts ticking again the prophetic events of the Old Testament will rapidly unfold. Israel and the church run on two tracks and always will.

This literalism also applies to chronology. The 1260 days of Daniel 7-9 and Revelation 11 are predictive prophecy. Contrary to the generally accepted notion that these numbers are symbols with a spiritual meaning, the Plymouth Brethren insisted that literal days are meant and applied them to future events of the coming tribulation period.

In the centuries of Christendom, "replacement theology" has generally been the prevailing view. It functioned with a vengeance in the crusades and the Spanish Inquisition. The first blood shed in the crusades was Jewish blood, as the crusaders marched through Germany on their way to free the holy places of Christendom from the Muslim infidels in1096. The Spanish Inquisition drove the last Jews out of Spain in 1492, and the royalty turned their attention to subsidizing Christopher Columbus and his voyages.

Joachim of Fiore, the twelfth century apocalyptist, believed that all Jews would be converted at the day of the Lord; however, before that time they would follow the Antichrist and bring terrible suffering upon themselves and the whole world. The idea that the Antichrist would be a Jew was a theme in late medieval mystery plays and took root in Catholic and Protestant thought. Early in the Reformation Martin Luther called attention to the fact that Jesus Christ was Jewish; however, when Jews did not respond in faith to the Gospel he wrote a negative treatise, *Von den Juden und ihren Lugen* ("Concerning the Jews and Their Lies"). In 1555 Pope Paul IV established a Jewish ghetto in Rome to facilitate conversion efforts.[4]

English Puritans took the prophecies of Israel's restoration literally, anticipating the Jews eventual conversion. Joseph Mede, for example, said that the Jews would accept Christianity and return to Judea to share in Christ's millennial kingdom. Oliver Cromwell spoke of it in a 1653 address to Parliament. The New England Puritans carried this doctrine to colonial America. In *The Mystery of Israel's Salvation Explained and Applied* (1669), Increase Mather taught that the Jews, after turning to Christ, would be brought back to their own land and found "the most glorious nation in the whole world."[5] The interest in Jewish restoration faded in the early part of the next century. Jonathan Edwards and other preachers in the first Great Awakening believed in a millennium, but thought it would occur in America rather than in Palestine. Edwards and later his grandson, Timothy Dwight, expressed a special interest in the year 2000 as the possible date for the beginning of the millennium.

The French Revolution sparked renewed interest in prophecy in England and the United States, including the future of the Jews. Politicians as well as preachers expressed their feelings. Near the end of his life, former President John Adams wrote, "I really wish the Jews again in Judea, an independent nation." In 1839, Lord Anthony Ashley Cooper, the Earl of Shaftesbury, argued that the Jewish return to Palestine must occur before the second coming of Christ. Through his influence England opened a consulate in Jerusalem; the consul general, an evangelical Christian, was given instructions to look out for the interests of the ten thousand Jews living in Palestine under Turkish Ottoman rule.[6]

At the same time, John Darby and the Plymouth Brethren were advancing their dispensational views in England and the United States. Prophecy conferences were organized and stimulated missionary work among Jews, often correlating conversion efforts with the theme of Jewish restoration to Israel. In 1878, William E. Blackstone (W.E.B.), an influential Chicago business man, wrote *Jesus Is Coming*, which became a best seller. In 1891 he urged President Benjamin Harrison to support a Jewish homeland in Palestine. He cited prophecy and argued that Palestine was the Jews' "inalienable possession, from which they were expelled by force."[7]

Six years later, in 1897, Theodore Herzl officially launched the Zionist movement at the first World Zionist Conference in Basel, Switzerland. Although Herzl and the early Zionists were secular Jews, Christian prophecy writers welcomed the development as a startling sign of the future. In spite of continuing efforts to convert Jews to Christ, Blackstone became good friends with Jewish Zionists. In 1918, at a Zionist conference in Philadelphia, Blackstone was honored as a "Father of Zionism."

World War I brought enormous changes in the Middle East. With the collapse of the Ottoman Empire, Palestine came under the British Mandate.

In 1917 Lord Arthur Balfour, the British Foreign Secretary, wrote to Lord James Rothschild, a Zionist leader: "His Majesty's Government views with favour the establishment in Palestine of a national home for the Jewish people, and will use their best efforts to facilitate the achievement of this object, it being clearly understood that nothing shall be done which may prejudice the civil and religious rights of existing non-Jewish communities in Palestine, or the rights and political status enjoyed by Jews in any other country."[8] A few weeks later British forces captured Jerusalem from the Turks.

Dispensationalists were ecstatic even though control of Jerusalem had passed to yet another Gentile nation. But the Balfour Declaration stated the British intentions. The "times of the Gentiles" were coming to an end.

The German Nazi party's rise to power in 1933 launched a series of tragic events. Hitler's goal to make Europe "Judenfrei" (free of Jews) resulted in the Holocaust. As the Nazi terror mounted, many Jews were leaving Germany, with substantial numbers going to Palestine. Arabs mounted strong resistance to this influx, with strikes and occasional terrorism. Caught between the Jews and Arabs, the British issued a white paper in 1939 that basically abandoned the Balfour Declaration.

With the end of World War II, the Jewish migration to Palestine became a flood, with increasing acts of terrorism by both sides. Desperate for a way out, the British appealed to the United Nations. In August, 1947 the UN Special Committee on Palestine (UNSCOP) recommended a partition into Arab and Jewish states. Arabs rejected the plan. With tensions rising, the British announced plans to withdraw their forces in Palestine on May 14, 1948. On that day the Jewish National Council, under the leadership of David Ben-Gurion, declared Israel's independence. The United States immediately recognized Israel. Several Arab armies invaded, determined to drive the outnumbered Jews into the sea. Fierce fighting followed, but the desperate Israeli forces prevailed and a cease fire was called. Israel had survived the first of five wars with Arab nations. In May1949, Israel was admitted to the United Nations.

Since the War of Independence (1948-49), Israel has fought four more wars as well as limited encounters that continue to the present time. In 1956 Israel, with French and English support, invaded Sinai. England and France wanted control of the Suez Canal; Israel wanted Sinai. The United States and the Soviet Union opposed the action and after a short conflict the invaders withdrew. Most dispensationalists opposed American policy, considering it to be anti-Israel. "For dispensationalists, not to support Israel was to align oneself *against* the purposes of God."[9]

The Six-Day War of June 1967 was a blitzkrieg conflict in which the Israeli forces routed the Arab coalition on three fronts. At the end of the brief conflict, Israel occupied the Sinai peninsula, the West Bank, Gaza, and the Golan Heights. The biggest prize was Israel's control of all of Jerusalem. For many, especially dispensationalists, the prophecy of Luke 21:24 was fulfilled: "Jerusalem will be trampled on by the Gentiles until the times of the Gentiles are fulfilled" (NRSV).

After 1967, the United States greatly increased its financial support of Israel. Powerful political support for this policy came not only from American Jews, but also from religious quarters. As pressure increased on Israel to make peace with its neighbors, an alliance was forming between the Israeli government and evangelicals. Israel's interests were security; evangelicals and dispensationalists focused on fulfilment of Bible prophecy. Fifteen hundred delegates from 32 countries attended a 1971 prophecy conference in Jerusalem, with Prime Minister David Ben-Gurion greeting the assembly. Large tour groups, led by Jerry Falwell, Oral Roberts, Hal Lindsey and others, were given briefings and favored treatment by the Israeli Ministry of Tourism.

In 1970 Hal Lindsey's best seller, *The Late Great Planet Earth,* introduced dispensationalism to millions.[10] By 1992 it had sold over 25 million copies. With his breezy style, Lindsey connected the dispensational chronology to current events. Drawing heavily on chapters from Daniel 7-9, Ezekiel 38-39, and Revelation, Lindsey put the jigsaw puzzle together in an entertaining yet scary scenario. As one student said to me in 1974, "He gets it all together!"

In this sensational book, Lindsey regards the 1960s—the drug culture, immorality, apostasy of mainline liberal religion—as a countdown to the last days. With Israel restored to the land, Lindsey believes that the Temple will be built on Mount Moriah in Jerusalem and the Mosaic sacrifices resumed. Meanwhile, a "Future Fuehrer" or Antichrist, joined by a False Prophet, will emerge and be widely worshiped during the Great Tribulation. He will rule over a revived Roman Empire consisting of a ten member European Common Market. The rapture will occur with Christ's first return. A northern confederacy, consisting of the Soviet Union and its eastern bloc (Gog and Magog), and a southern Arab-African coalition led by Egypt will invade Israel, "the fuse of Armageddon." They will be joined by a 200 million member army from Red China. The world's final battle of Armageddon will be fought—involving terrible suffering for Israel before divine intervention saves it. The invaders will be destroyed but nuclear destruction will be worldwide. At the climax of this hellish war, Jesus Christ will return and save humanity from self-extinction. He will rule over the nations for a thousand years from the throne of David in Jerusalem, with the Jewish people converting and worshiping Jesus as Messiah.

Bible prophecy has had important political consequences. With the success of *The Late Great Planet Earth*, Lindsey was invited to speak at Bible prophecy meetings, the American Air War College and even with Israeli government officials. After the Six Day War, evangelicals organized Christians Concerned for Israel, which later changed its name to the National Christian Leadership Conference for Israel (NCLCI). It defended Israel's invasion of Lebanon in 1982, even though many Israelis opposed that war. The NCLCI has resisted any attempt to internationalize Jerusalem or to trade West Bank land (Judea and

Samaria) for peace with the Palestinians, even opposing American government policy on the latter issue.

Evangelicals in general, and dispensationalists in particular, profess to have a high view of inspired Scripture. The militant Messianists, like Jerry Falwell and Pat Robertson, make no objections to Israeli oppression of Palestinians: beatings and unwarranted arrests, land appropriations, illegal settlements, etc. These and other actions are justified in the name of Israeli security. To criticize Israel is to oppose God! But even as the prophets held ancient Israel accountable, is not modern Israel also answerable for its actions? Is not the Lord who meets us in the Scriptures a God of profound justice? Is not this Lord a God of peace? And is not peace with justice *for all people*, Jews and Palestinians, God's will? Do not the Scriptures, Old and New Testament, witness to this prophetic vision? Here is an example where a professed high view of Scripture and faithfulness to the biblical content are in inverse ratio!

RESPONSE

The sale of books by Hal Lindsey, John Walvoord, Salem Kirban, and others demonstrates the continuing interest in and influence of dispensationalism with millions of Americans. For some it provides answers to their curiosity about the future and the end of time. For others it gives courage and emotional certainty in the face of the future. It is like a roller coaster ride, scary but you know the outcome.

Darbyism, or dispensationalism, had a rapid growth in the American post-Civil War period, a time of accelerating cultural and religious change. It was contemporary with the spread of Charles Darwin's evolutionary thought and the beginning of biblical higher criticism in liberal Protestant seminaries. Both were threatening developments to traditional Christians, and a prelude to the controversies that divided denominations in the 1920s.

American historian George M. Marsden stated that "dispensationalist thought was characterized by a dual emphasis on the supernatural and the scientific."[11] The supernatural is evident with the emphasis on angels, heavens, and the conflict between God and Satan. To an outsider, the scientific element would not be so obvious. However, as one representative stated, dispensationalism is a scientific enterprise along the lines of "a Baconian system . . . (it) first gathers the teachings of the word of God, and then seeks to deduce some general law upon which the facts can be arranged."[12]

Dispensationalists are convinced that they are taking the facts of authoritative and inerrant Scripture, arranging and integrating them into a precise system that is reinforced by proof texts. When the Bible is regarded as the perfect and predestined design of God, every detail is significant and true. Scripture does not deviate from exact truth. The implications for interpreting the Bible are obvious. Precise numbers of years must be calculated and correlated with historical events. The millennium means exactly one thousand years; 70 weeks (Daniel 9) is a literal 490 years.

However, there is an Achilles heel in this method. Interpreting prophecy belief historically undermines a basic assumption of dispensationalists—that the signs of the time are valid because they are signs of *this time* and no other. For Scofield and Lindsey, Gog refers to Russia. Two centuries earlier, some scholars had referred to Gog as the Ottoman empire, also north of Palestine. With the collapse of the Soviet Union and the current weakness of Russia, must another interpretation be made? Or should we set our study of Ezekiel within the sixth century B.C. context when he lived and prophesied?

This leads to a consideration of literary classifications or literary genres. The main sources of dispensationalists for constructing their system are the Old Testament prophets and the book of Revelation. Of individual books, Ezekiel, Daniel, and Revelation are most frequently quoted. While Daniel is listed with the four major prophets in English Bibles, it is placed with the "Writings" (*kethubim*) in the Hebrew Bible. Hal Lindsey makes several references to "the prophet Daniel." This is incorrect; Daniel and Revelation belong to the apocalyptic genre, and there are over a dozen apocalyptic writings in the Old Testament pseudepigrapha.[13] There is also the apocalyptic II Esdras, part of the New Testament apocrypha, as well as the War Scroll

("The War of the Sons of Light and the Sons of Darkness," an apocalyptic writing in the Dead Sea Scriptures from Qumran.) Dispensationalist writers seem to be unaware of this literature.

Unfortunately the book of Revelation has been the happy hunting ground for predictive sharpshooters building their timetable of future events. Revelation deserves better consideration than this. The opening line gives us a clue to reading it: "The revelation (apocalypse) of Jesus Christ." This states the theme which is the heartbeat of the book. Jesus Christ is revealing himself to his church which is enduring persecution for his name, this is a vision of hope for his suffering church. We usually refer to Revelation as a book, though in literary form it is a letter, actually a series of letters to seven churches (Revelation 2—3). And in addressing seven churches, Jesus is speaking to the whole catholic church. Revelation then is a book of the church, and was meant to be read aloud in the worship service of the congregations.

The Old Testament prophetic books, from Isaiah to Malachi, are a distinct genre. They originated over a four to five hundred year period of ancient Hebrew history and should be studied and interpreted within that context. While there are rhetorical features in common with other neighboring cultures, the message of the prophets is quite unique. The prophets were primarily *forthtellers*, speaking forth the will of God to Israel in their time. They drew upon a covenant tradition that was hundreds of years deep. Yahweh had called Israel into a special covenant relationship, with promises and warnings. The prophets were primarily *foretellers* of the future. When they did predict future events it was with reference to promise or judgment upon people or nations, including Israel. To regard them as predictive sharpshooters of events twenty-five hundred years later is at best, inaccurate and misleading, and at worst "horrible hermeneutics."

The strong orientation toward the written word of the Bible partially explains the literalism of dispensationalists. The plain literal meaning was consistent with common sense, as opposed to flowery illustrations and poetic metaphor. Symbolic and allegorical language with hidden or secret meanings was strongly suspect. But what about symbolism in the book of Revelation, particularly with reference to the number seven? In addition to the seven churches, there are seven beatitudes, seven spirits before the throne, seven seals, seven trumpets, and seven bowls of wrath. Seven is fundamental to the structure of Revelation and also to its message. In the letters to seven churches the whole catholic church is addressed. As the drama develops, there is a strange play upon the numbers six and seven. The seven plagues released at the trumpet blasts are really six plus one. In that extra one, six woes are revealed that are in effect a repetition of the first six. Then there is the seventh in which six vials of wrath are poured out, plus one more. At each stage, the seventh indicates that the plagues and woes and tribulations are in the hand of God. In the seventh plague or seventh woe or seventh vial of wrath, God intervenes in final judgment. Evil always falls short and fails. "It was and is not . . . and goes to perdition" (17:11).

Carried to an extreme, literalism gets ridiculous. There is the wry joke about the rationalist who detested the mysterious and spent his energy translating poetry into prose. Concerning symbolic language, Austin Farrer has written: "We write in symbol when we wish our words to present, rather than analyse or prove, their subject-matter. . . . Symbol endeavors, as it were, to *be* that of which it speaks. . . . There is a current and exceedingly stupid doctrine that symbol evokes emotion, and exact prose states reality. . . . Nothing could be further from the truth; exact prose abstracts from reality, symbol presents it."[14]

Concerning cosmology, it is puzzling that those who insist on being precise and even scientific in Scripture interpretation, on the one hand, hold to a literal rapture of believers into the heavens, on the other hand. Of course the writers of the Bible reflected the ancient geocentric cosmology with a three-story view of the universe. This was their world view. The apostle Paul, for example, might have considered heaven as thousands of miles in the sky, but his pastoral concern was not space or altitude, but the nature of life *with the Lord* (I Thessalonians 4:17). In the second millennium, we have gone through several world views—from geocentric to heliocentric to island galaxies to an ever- expanding universe. Lest we get too arrogant about our scientific knowledge, what will be the world view in another 500 years?

Theologically, there seems to be little emphasis on the incarnation and the resurrection in dispensationalist theology. Christ's radical claim to bring in the kingdom through exorcisms is given scant attention (Luke 11:20=Matthew 12:28). And the sharp separation between Israel and the church in God's redemptive plan is biblically impossible. It rests upon Darby's and Scofield's unscriptural distinction between "the kingdom of heaven" and "the kingdom of God." In the New Testament, both mean the rule of God, only the wording is different. Writing for a Jewish community of believers who hesitated to even mention the divine name, Matthew consistently wrote "kingdom of heaven." "Kingdom of God" occurs frequently in Mark and Luke, and a few times in the Gospel of John and the letters of Paul.

The New Testament clearly states that the church of believing Jews and Gentiles is now the spiritual Israel. Paul writes that the middle wall of partition between Jew and and Gentile has been broken down (Ephesians 2:14), that God has reconciled both Jews and Gentiles unto himself "in one body" (2:16), and Gentiles are members of the same household of God (2:19). In Romans 11:17-24 Paul states the relationship with an allegory of the olive tree: the root and branches represent Israel, the wild branches grafted in are the believing Gentiles who have come lately into the faith. The fellowship is not two trees (one Jewish and one Gentile) but *one olive tree.* And Peter, quoting Exodus 19:5-6, addresses a church of Jews and Gentiles as "a chosen race, a royal priesthood, a holy nation, God's own people" (I Peter 2:9).

In Christian charity, it would be unfair to conclude this chapter without two or three favorable comments about dispensationalist believers. In general, they have been zealous in evangelism and winning converts. In spite of his razzle-dazzle style, Hal Lindsey's writings have an evangelistic purpose—accept Christ before it is too late. Turn or burn! In global missionary work, they have been faithful to preach the Gospel to all nations. And in spite of the strange teaching of the rapture, many have been and continue to be faithful workers in programs that preserve and improve society. It is their biblical method and theological conclusions that are unconvincing. But let us remember that in the end we are not saved by our theology, but by God's grace.

Chapter 4

CHE YEAR OF JUBILEE

The Year of Jubilee is a legacy of Hebrew life and worship. Jubilee is the biblical alternative to an escapist rapture mentality. Though it may seem utopian in our pluralistic society, its principles would have a salutary effect for life in the next millennium: rest and leisure, ecology and care of the earth, prison reform, and economic and social justice. Jubilee affirms life on earth as God's gift and calls believers to responsible stewardship and thanksgiving.

REMEMBER THE SABBATH DAY

Among the people of the ancient world, the Israelites were unique in their observance of the Sabbath. The creation and Sabbath traditions were generations older, but were sensitized and shaped during and after the exile in Babylon. With the deportation in 587 B.C., the exiled Israelites found themselves living in an advanced culture but a heathen environment. "By the rivers of Babylon there we sat down and there we wept when we remembered Zion" (Psalm 137:1). Memory and challenge! In Babylon their understanding of God, of creation and the Sabbath were challenged, honed, and refined.

Genesis 1:1-2:4a is a grand creation hymn. It is a song of praise for God's power and generosity. The preface (1:1-3) proclaims God's act of creation and power over chaos. It is followed by six majestic stanzas (1:4-31) wherein the priestly poet(s), with rhythm and repetition, celebrate the drama, order, and power of the Creator's unfolding purpose. "And God said, 'Let there be.' . . . 'And it was so.' . . . 'And God saw that it was good.' . . . 'And there was evening and morning, the . . . day.'" On the sixth day, God made humankind (Hebrew, *adham*—male and female) in his image, blessed them, giving them dominion as God's representatives, over the rest of the creatures. The blessing endows the creatures, including "adham," with vitality and fruitfulness. In six days, God has created *by his word*, the heavens and earth and the creatures in it. The structure is complete. " And God saw everything that he had made, and indeed, it was *very good*" (1:31). It was "very good"—for God's purpose!

The contrast of the Genesis creation hymn and the Babylonian creation myth is striking. Instead of a dozen gods, there is one supreme God. Where there is creation by war between the gods, God creates by his word. In the Babylonian account, humans are created from the blood of the monster; in Genesis 1:27, *adham* (male and female) is created "in the image of God," to be God's representative on earth. We usually, and mistakenly, speak of six days of creation. However, the creation drama continues on the seventh day (Genesis 2:1-4a). (The chapter division of the priestly account, made centuries after the original text, is unfortunate.) Creation of the heavens and earth was "finished" (2:1). "And on the seventh day God *finished* his work . . . and he *rested* on the seventh day. . . . God *blessed* the seventh day and *hallowed* it" (2:2-3).

The creation actually culminates on the seventh day with the institution of the sabbath. God *finished* his work and *rested* (Hebrew "*shabat*"). Unlike the restless, clawing, and warring Babylonian deities, God spends the day in serenity and peace. God blesses and hallows it; it is a gracious turning toward the creation and the creatures in it. The world is safely in God's hands!

To regard the seventh day and the sabbath as the culmination of God's creation flies in the face of most European and North American interpretations. The latter view regards the creation of humankind on the sixth day and the command to have dominion over the earth and other creatures as the climax of God's creative activity. However, according to Larry Rasmussen, "in the (Jewish) rabbinical tradition, it is Sabbath and not dominion that symbolizes the proper relationship of humans to the rest of nature and of all creation together to the creator. Indeed, Sabbath, and not the creation of humans, is the crown and climax of the creation story itself, papal exegesis notwithstanding."[1] At the World Council of Churches Assembly in Canberra, Australia, in 1991, delegates from the Third World countries, reacting to colonialism, generally supported the stewardship model rather than the dominion model in the discussions.[2]

Remember! "Remember the sabbath day, and keep it holy" (Exodus 20:8). We memorized that line as one of the Ten Commandments, but the text continues: "Six days you shall labor and do all your work. But the seventh day is a sabbath to the Lord your God; you shall not do any work—you, your son or your daughter, your male or female slave, your livestock, or the alien resident in your towns. For in six days the Lord made heaven and earth, the sea, and all that is in them, but rested the seventh day; therefore, the Lord blessed the seventh day and consecrated it" (Exodus 20:9-11).

Work and worship, labor and leisure, activity and rest make up our natural rhythm of human existence. Children roam and play in the day and sleep at night. Normally adults do too, except for college students! On the sabbath God rests, and also the creatures, including your ox, your ass, your cattle (Deuteronomy 5:14, RSV).

"Sabbath is the end of grasping and therefore the end of exploitation. Sabbath is a day of revolutionary equality in society. On that day all rest equally, regardless of wealth or power or need."[3]

In Babylon, observing the sabbath became a "status confessionis" (G. von Rad)—a sign of the covenant for Israel. Along with circumcision, it set the Israelites apart from other people. Sabbath was an event that announced faith in the covenant God and a rejection of other gods and religions. Sabbath celebration of the seventh day became a declaration of trust in the God who blessed and hallowed a day of rest.

New challenges confronted the returning exiles from Babylon in 536 B.C . Jerusalem and the temple were in ruins, and the prophets Haggai and Zechariah stirred up the people to a rebuilding program. According to the fifth century prophet

Malachi, who was last in the prophetic line, there was laxity and abuse in worship. Decades later the priest Ezra led a reform in which marriages with heathen women were dissolved and sabbath worship regulated and enforced (Nehemiah 13:15-23). Israel's unique identity as "a priestly kingdom and a holy nation" (Exodus 19:6) was preserved. Through the centuries even to the present in Jewish homes, the day of rest commences on Friday evening with the words "Blessed are you Lord God, King of the universe, who has ordained for us the sabbath."

"Remember the sabbath day, and keep it holy." We live in the most anti-sabbath society in the world. Stores boast, with no apology, that they are open 365 days a year. In the business of modern life we have lost the rhythm between action and rest. Even in secularized western Europe, stores are closed from Saturday noon to Monday morning. But not in the good old USA, where I can "shop 'til I drop" seven days a week! And this has generally happened in the last several decades of the twentieth century. The Sunday openings started more slowly in many communities, gradually expanding, like a camel getting its nose under the tent.

The mall is more and more becoming the American cathedral. Several years ago the largest local mall, with some 300 stores, announced it was changing its Sunday opening hours from noon to 11 A.M. Pulling clergy rank, I sent a letter to the manager, explaining that this might interfere with workers' family schedules and also worship opportunities. The reply, in summary, was polite and self-serving! Thank you for writing. It is not our intention to disrupt family plans or keep employees from church. However, the earlier opening hour of this shopping mall is merely following the national trend. One is reminded of the merchants whom the eighth century prophet Amos indicted: "When will the new moon be over so that we may sell grain; and the sabbath, so that we may offer wheat for sale?" (8:5).

We could learn from our Jewish friends. Walking the streets of west Jerusalem on a Saturday morning is a lesson in sabbath. Every store and shop is closed. Streets and sidewalks are virtually empty. Buses and taxis aren't running. All is quiet, except for the birds. Sabbath rest!

One expression of renewal for Christians in the next millennium would be to "do sabbath." For most Christians Sunday is that day of rest and worship, though every day is holy when remembered as a day of God's grace and mercy. "Remember the sabbath and keep it holy." Our culture is loaded with a spiritual vacuum. The eternal advertisements, the grabbing and greed, and the relentless pace are responses to this condition.

Jesus knew how to keep sabbath. He called his disciples to come away from the crowds and rest and pray for a while. Back with the multitudes he cut through legalistic scribal rules to heal hurting humans, even on the sabbath, for he was "Lord of the sabbath" (Mark 2:28). Rest! Pray! Take a walk alone or with a friend. Visit a shut-in. Make a hospital call. Have a restful and refreshing meal with family. And may it begin with a blessing like our family has used for decades: "Come Lord Jesus, be our guest, and let these gifts to us be blessed."

LAND SABBATH

There is a thin layer of land that surrounds the earth and forms a bridge between food and famine, life and death for the families of the world. Whenever such issues are involved, God is there. That is why the Bible has much to say about the land.

In Leviticus 25:1-7 the sabbath rest is extended to the land. After six years of working the fields and tending the vineyards, the land should rest. The same rule is stated in Exodus 23:10-11:

> For six years you shall sow your land and gather
> in its yield; but the seventh year you shall let it
> rest and lie fallow, so that the poor of your people
> may eat; and what they leave, the wild animals
> may eat.

In Exodus the motive is humanitarian, a concern for the poor which also extended to wild animals. (Incidentally, how much concern other than economic is given to animals and poultry in modern agri-business?) In Leviticus the motive is primarily religious: "the land shall observe a sabbath for the Lord" (25:2b).

The Lord owns the land and gives it to his people for stewardship. The gift bound Israel in new ways to the Giver. When Israel was in Egypt's land, it was landless and enslaved; it was "not a people." At the boundary to the land of promise Israel was told to *listen* to the Lord: "*Hear* (Hebrew, "*shema*") O Israel: the Lord our God is one Lord; and you shall love the Lord your God with all your heart, and with all your soul, and with all your might" (Deuteronomy 6:4,5, RSV). *Yes* to the Lord; *no* to the fertility gods of Baal.

Once in the land, the people and land would observe sabbath, "a sabbath for the Lord." The right to the land and its products, originally granted by God, reverted back to the Giver during the seventh year. By God's decree all work on the land was suspended: no sowing, no harvesting, no pruning. The effect was to establish an equality between the rich and the poor in matters of sustenance.

The prohibition on sowing and harvesting in verses 4 and 5 is modified in verses 6 and 7. This appears to accommodate the law to difficult circumstances. When necessary, the volunteer crop could be harvested so that all people and animals might have food. Furthermore, anxieties about scarcity are addressed in Leviticus 25:20-22, where God promises his blessing and a bumper crop in the sixth year which would be sufficient for three years.

Was the land sabbath kept in ancient Israel? There is a reference from the chronicler of observance during the exile (II Chronicles 36:21). The Jewish historian Josephus states that the seventh year fallowing was kept by Jews and Samaritans at the time of Alexander the Great (*Antiquities* XI, viii. 6), and also observed in the time of the Maccabees and Herod (*Antiquities* XIX, xvi.2). There is reference to a food shortage in a sabbatical year during one of the Maccabean wars (I Maccabees 6:49-54). It was likely observed, though perhaps not universally.

What message does land sabbath have for modern urbanized and industrialized America? At the end of World War I, one in four Americans was engaged in agriculture while today only one in fifty is so occupied. Yet the 2% in farming produce food for the rest of the citizens and for a large export market.

This is a modern success story and a witness to the world of American productivity and efficiency.

Fewer farmers feeding more and more people! It is a marriage of industry and technology, on the one hand, and agriculture, on the other hand. But lest we forget, agriculture is primary, industry is secondary! Lose the land, and you lose life! For productivity and sustainability there must be a balance of the two. And farmers, urbanites, professional economists, scientists, politicians, teachers, preachers and the like should acknowledge this. How many urban people think that milk and beef come only from the grocery store? How many economists and politicians consider that two bushels of Iowa top soil is lost for every bushel of corn produced? How many preachers give an "Earth Day" sermon to their urban or suburban congregations?

The crude materialistic view thinks of agriculture as directed basically toward food production. This is frontier economics in a postfrontier world. A wider view of the land as a priceless resource, a garden which "adham" is "to till and to keep" (Genesis 2:15) is essential. Human management of the land must involve three goals—health, beauty, and permanence—and then productivity will be attained as a by-product.[4]

Think of the land as alive. A cubic yard of fertile and healthy soil contains countless living organisms. According to Aldo Leopold in his classic *A Sand County Almanac,*[5] the outstanding scientific discovery of the twentieth century is not radio or TV, but the complexity of the land organism. The frontier men who cut the trees, cleared the brush, and plowed the virgin soil could not have known this. It required the modern microscope and research in soil science to discover the existence of these "small cogs and wheels" in the land's biotic community. Little things move the earth! The process of nature's building this community has taken millenia, even aeons, of time. The ultimate word in stupidity is to say of a handful of soil: "It's only dirt!"

The poet who wrote that "beauty has its own excuse for being" expressesd a marvelous truth. The beauty of the earth, its land and water and sky, is too grand to waste on a prose discussion. It is to be experienced and expressed in poetry and song. I read that Katherine Lee Bates was inspired to write "America the Beautiful" during a visit to Pike's Peak in Colorado. The list of awe- inspiring scenes is endless: the Boundary Waters of Minnesota and Ontario, Glacier and Yellowstone and Yosemite National Parks, the Black Hills of South Dakota, the lakes and woods of Wisconsin, the redwood trees in California, the Blue Ridge mountains of Virginia, the Amish farms of Lancaster County in Pennsylvania, and the "amber fields of grain" from Texas to North Dakota and north into Canada. And Aldo Leopold, writing about the loss of wilderness, urged preservation of plots of long-grass prairie, virgin pineries of the Great Lakes, hardwoods of the Appalachians, and flatwoods of the coastal plain. The larger expanses of virgin wilderness area in Canada and Alaska can and should be kept.[6]

It is an understatement to say that there has been a revolution in agriculture in the twentieth century. Ol' Dobbin was put out to pasture and replaced with the tractor. In the decades that followed, the changes accelerated with larger and heavier machinery. The bigger and heavier they are the more the soil is compacted. After World War II, chemical fertilizers, pesticides and herbicides were increasingly applied to the land. With these products and hybrid seeds, yields have doubled and even tripled. But what is heavy machinery and continuing use of chemicals doing to the living biotic community in the soil? Where are the earthworms?

Modern methods of agriculture have been used on my home farm for a number of years. When I was a youngster we used a four-five year rotation of corn, small grain, hay—usually alfalfa, and pasture. The land was fertilized with some lime and barnyard manure. There was no problem finding earthworms for fishing bait?

On one of my last visits to the farm, which is no longer in the family, I went digging for worms to no avail. Where are the earthworms?

Is modern agriculture sustainable through the next century? And through the next millennium?

I know several land owners who do organic farming. One in particular, a South Dakota farmer, has a six-year rotation program. "It is more work but it is worth it," says Charlie. The yield may not be quite as great but his organically grown soybeans are sold for better prices. He also writes poetry about the land. He has been politically involved in the effort to limit the spread of large hog feedlots in the state. And yes, he sets aside a number of acres each year for "God's acres." Before planting, his bishop or a priest blesses the seed and the land. After harvest, the crop is sold and the money given to the parochial school his children attend, the Catholic church to which his family belongs, and a neighboring Lutheran church. This is "land sabbath."

For too long we have measured progress and success by an increasing Gross National Product as though land and environment did not matter. Perhaps you have heard the argument that agriculture and forestry are not particularly important since they make up only three percent of the U. S. economy. This is like saying that the heart, since it is only one to two percent of body weight, is insignificant to one's health and well-being.

Chief Seattle, chief of the Suquamish and Duwamish tribes of the Pacific northwest and a Roman Catholic convert, said of the earth: "This we know. . . . The earth does not belong to man; man belongs to the earth. All things are connected like the blood that unites us all. Man did not weave the web of life; he is merely a strand of it. Whatever he does to the web, he does to himself."[7]

Former Senator Gaylord Nelson, originator of Earth Day in 1970 and at 82 still working with the Wilderness Society, warns about exploiting natural resources for profit. Fifty years ago, Aldo Leopold wrote that the "key-log" in a land ethic is to quit thinking about decent land use as solely economic. "A thing is right when it tends to preserve the integrity, stability, and beauty of the biotic community. It is wrong when it tends otherwise."[8] Where there is a will there is a way. The United States, so richly endowed, can care for its land and keep it healthy and beautiful into the next millennium.

THE YEAR OF JUBILEE

In ancient Israel, every fiftieth year was the Year of Jubilee. This was the "sabbath of sabbaths." "You shall count off seven weeks of years, seven times seven years, so that the period of seven weeks of years gives forty-nine years" (Leviticus 25:8). The word "jubilee" is derived from the Hebrew "yobhel," which is a ram's horn. It was the Year of the Ram, the year of the blowing of the ram's horn, the trumpet in ancient Israel. The trumpet was to be blown on the tenth day of the seventh month, which is the day of atonement (Hebrew, "*Yom Kippur*"). This was and still is the great penitential day of the Hebrew calendar. In modern Israel, even secular Jews go to pray in the synagogue on Yom Kippur.

The ritual for the day of atonement is described in Leviticus 16. This significant event is the context for the Holiness Code, a body of laws and regulations in Leviticus 17-26. The theme that runs through these chapters like a red thread is God's word to Israel: "You shall be holy, for I the Lord your God am holy" (Leviticus 19:2). Within this "formula for sanctification," a variety of related subjects are considered: laws regarding priests and sacrifices, principles and laws of morality, and a sacred calendar of annual holy days concluding with the sabbatical year and the jubilee year (Leviticus 25).

Historically, it is not clear to what extent the jubilee year was observed. Like the sabbatical year, there should be no sowing or reaping or harvesting. Could Israel survive two years without normal crop production? But the principles involved in the jubilee are basic to the Old Testament concept of land and property and people, as well as significant themes in Jesus' ministry (esp. Luke 4:16 ff.).

The first principle is that *God owns the land.* "The land shall not be sold in perpetuity, for the land is mine; with me you are but aliens and tenants" (Leviticus 25:23). Such a declaration was fairly common in the ancient Orient. The land, along with flocks and herds, was the source of capital. Generally, in ancient countries the land belonged to the god of the area or the country. In practice, this meant it belonged either to the priests of the god or to the king that incarnated the god. The king or pharaoh, who had absolute authority, then granted the use of the lands to whomever he pleased.

It is remarkable in Israel that land use did not work out in an arbitrary way to the benefit of the king. The selfishness of the earthly sovereign was limited by provisions of the jubilee year. Every fiftieth year the family regained the land that it previously owned and might have lost during the interval. The story of Naboth's vineyard is most revealing. Naboth refused a seemingly fair purchase offer for his vineyard from King Ahab: "The Lord forbid that I should give you my ancestral inheritance" (I Kings 21:3). Naboth knew by established legal and religious custom that ancestral property must remain in the family in perpetuity (Leviticus 25:10, 13-17, 23-24, 34). Ahab knew this too and when his offer was refused he, like a pouting child, went to bed without his supper. His wife Jezebel, from a Phoenician culture, had no respect for the laws and religion of Israel. She manipulated events through a kangaroo court and two false witnesses that resulted in Naboth being stoned and Ahab taking possession of the vineyard. But God, who is not mocked, sent his prophet Elijah to Ahab with the fearful news of judgment upon the king and queen (I Kings 21:17ff.)

The second principle is that *God is the Liberator of his people.* "I am the Lord your God, who brought you out of the land of Egypt, to give you the land of Canaan, to be your God" (Leviticus 25:38). Note the direct address. Because God has set you free from Egyptian bondage by a liberating act, liberation from slavery and from debts will have the force of law among you. Blow the trumpet and "proclaim liberty throughout the land to all its inhabitants" (Leviticus 25:10). (It is interesting that "proclaim liberty throughout the land" is inscribed on the American Liberty Bell.) Remembering God's liberating action is justification for the Sabbath: "Remember that you were a slave in the land of Egypt, and the Lord your God brought you out from there with a mighty hand and an outstretched arm; therefore the Lord your God commanded you to keep the sabbath day" (Deuteronomy 5:15).

These principles were the basis for the specific provisions of the jubilee year that Israel was called to hallow and observe.

Old debts were cancelled out. Imagine the thrill of the small landowner who was on the verge of losing his property, but then learned that his large debt has been forgiven! However, in practice it might not have been quite that simple. As the jubilee year neared it apparently had the unhappy side effect of freezing credit (see Deuteronomy 15:7-11). Wealthy people were more reluctant to loan money to the poor. By the time of Jesus even some champions of the law, including Hillel and Shammai, were hesitant about a strict application of its provisions. Those with resources found a way whereby loans could be collected, even with interest; this was known as "*prosboul*" and led to the rich devouring the poor. This was one of the charges that Jesus made when he accused the Pharisees of devouring widows' houses (Matthew 23:14).

The Year of Jubilee called Israel to remembrance—of sabbath and of deliverance from bondage. It was a moment of justice, a sabbatical period to regularize the relations between God and his liberated people. It remains uncertain to what extent the jubilee was observed in Israel. What is certain is that God looks out for people, particularly the poor of the land. In practice, the Year of Jubilee may be summarized as follows: 1) the forgiveness of old debts, 2) the liberation or redemption of slaves, and 3) the redistribution of capital.

RETURN TO ANCESTRAL LAND

At the end of the forty-ninth year from the previous jubilee the ram's horn, or shofar, was sounded on the Day of Atonement to announce the beginning of the new jubilee year. The two consecutive years, the sabbatical and the jubilee, were a special time of blessing and renewal. Most Israelites would celebrate this occasion with their families at least once in a lifetime.

The sounding of the shofar signalled a jubilee return and release. It was comprehensive, including the return to ancestral land and property as well as the release of indebted servants. "It shall be a jubilee for you: and you shall return, every one of you to your property and every one of you to your family" (Leviticus 25:10b, 13). Land and its resources is the basis for wealth and survival. Most Americans regard private owner-ship of land and property as the norm. However, most native American tribes do not recognize private ownership but rather claim tribal rights to the territory in which members reside. This is a significant cultural difference. Certain white Ameri-cans have even said that Indians should introduce private own-ership if they want to become real human beings!

The land ethic in ancient Israel rested on a religious premise within the Holiness Code. Consequently it was radically differ-ent from current westernized ideas and laws. Israelites were "aliens and tenants" on land that did not belong to them by right but which the Lord had given them as an inheritance. Therefore land was not to be sold "in perpetuity" (25:23). Land was held in common by a family as a trust, and no individual could speculate with it or sell it for profit. We recall Naboth's reply to Ahab concerning his ancestral inheritance (I Kings 21:3).

The return to the ancestral land was a new beginning for families that had been forced off the property in the interven-ing 49 years. Living off the land was a tenuous and risky exist-ence. Wars, droughts, storms, thefts, and other threats made life a gamble. Taxes on mortgaged land were almost impossible to retire and will be discussed in the next section. The one hope for landless people was that every 50 years the lost prop-erty would revert back to them as descendants of the original residents. It was a social and economic program of redistribut-ing accumulated wealth and giving the poor an opportunity for a new life.

In the more developed economy of the monarchy some modifications were made in the laws concerning land and prop-erty. Under certain conditions property could be sold, but al-ways with the right of a family member to redeem it or buy it back (Leviticus 25:25-28 as well as other rules in the Holiness Code). Dishonesty in commercial transactions was an injustice to all society, but especially to the poor. Israelites who had fallen into poverty were to be supported; no interest was to be charged on loans (25:35-38). Although a man was forbidden to sell prop-erty in perpetuity, he could lease it for farming. In those in-stances, the rent was reckoned at the approximate value of the crops in the remaining years of the jubilee period (25:13-16). The longer it was before jubilee, the higher the price; the closer to jubilee, the lower the price. Cheating one another was strictly forbidden, "for I am the Lord your God" (25:17; 19:35-38).

A hired man was to be paid his wages daily so that he would have food for that day (19:13; compare the parable of the workers in the vineyard, Matthew 20:1-16).

The defense of the poor in the Holiness Code of Leviticus was grounded in God's covenant election of Israel. The prophets of Israel, from the eighth to the fifth centuries, drew from the same covenant source to indict people for their sins against God and the "have-nots" in Israel: unjust courts (Amos 5:12; Isaiah 10:1-2; Jeremiah 5:28); cheating in trade (Amos 8:4-5, Deuteronomy 25:13-15); theft of land (Micah 2:1-3); violence against the poor (Ezekiel 16:48); oppression of the poor by elders and leaders (Isaiah 3:13-15); cheating in sacrifices by the priests (Malachi 1:6-2:9). The list could go on and on. In Leviticus and Deuteronomy and the prophetic literature God is consistently defending the poor of the land against the powerful oppressors.

A distinction was made in Leviticus 25:29-31 between urban and open country. There were different laws for urban property than for agricultural land. Walled cities, typical of Canaanite city culture, were a novelty to Israel's early population, and their family law did not provide for them. A house in such a town was more an individual than a family possession. The right of redemption applied for a full year, but if it was not redeemed in that time it would pass in perpetuity to the purchaser and did not revert even in the jubilee year. But the houses in unwalled towns, where Israelites customarily lived, were considered landed property, and the old rules applied.

The Levites were a special case. As ministers who performed certain sanctuary duties, they were subordinate to the priests. They had no landed property of their own. In the course of Israel's history they were allotted a number of cities in which to reside (Joshua 21). These were held as a trust from God and consequently were "holy" and their possession for all time.

To what extent was the law of return to ancestral land observed?

In Numbers 27 and 36 we have the case of Zelophehad, who had five daughters but no sons. Tragic, because according to Israeli law women could not inherit or own property. Yet inheritance must remain in the family. The case set a precedent, and the order of inheritance was determined as daughters, brothers, father's brothers, and next of kin. So the daughters of Zelophehad inherited the property on condition that they marry within the family of their father's tribe. The inheritance must remain in the family tribe and not be transferred from one tribe to another.

Note that the jubilee is specifically mentioned in Numbers 36:4. When the law of return was implemented, as in the Zelophehad family, it became the most effective means of saving family property and redistributing wealth. Isaiah pronounced "woe" (RSV) on those who added "house to house" and "field to field" (Isaiah 5:8). What does God think of the American social and economic structure, in which the top one percent own 40 percent of the assets and the bottom 20 percent own five percent? Concerning Denmark's society, the nineteenth century Danish bishop and reformer N. F. S. Grundtvig wrote: "Then will we have achieved great wealth, when few have too much, and fewer (still) too little."

The current trends in American land ownership and management are disturbing. In the last half century the size of farms has been increasing, aided by larger farm machinery and new technologies of plant production. But farmers are still needed to plant and harvest the crop. The United States is losing them at an alarming rate, not just small operators or those reaching retirement age but farmers in their mid-forties who are calling it quits. And there is grief and pain that so often accompanies this decision. Furthermore, when rural young people consider the huge investment, low prices, and the long hours of work, most are opting for other vocations. The average age of the American farmer is now 53 years. Who will work the land and feed the country if and when this human resource is lost?

There are those who say agri-business corporations are the alternative. But why would they get involved in a losing enterprise, unless it is to corner the nation's food supply and hike prices? And will corporations "tend the garden" (Wesley Granberg-Michaelson) like the "dirt farmer" who lives on and loves the land? Wendell Berry wrote: "Contrary to popular assumption, good farmers are not in any simple way part of the 'labor force.' Good farmers, like good musicians, must be raised to the trade."[9]

In the Yahwist creation narrative the Lord God took the man and put him in the garden to till and keep it (Genesis 2:15). This means watchful care and preserving the good land and its resources. This requires humility, mystery, wonder, and awe toward God's world. In a word this means "bonding" with the land! And thanksgiving to and praise of the Creator! And actions that match!

RELEASE TO THE CAPTIVES

Slavery has been practiced in every type of society from antiquity to the modern age. The main reasons for slavery were punishment for wrong-doing and filling the demand for cheap labor. The oldest formal slave laws date from the Sumerians who lived in Mesopotamia before 2000 B.C. They show certain humane features that characterize later codes, including the Code of Hammurabi from 18th century ancient Babylon. Hammurabi's code allowed slaves certain legal rights. For example, slaves could be liberated with purchase by a free person, by self-purchase, by adoption, or by a master voluntarily setting them free. The freed slaves could then engage in business, own property, marry and raise their children as free citizens.

The civil laws of the Hebrews in the Old Testament, which are centuries later, share some interesting similarities with Hammurabi's code. Both have features protecting the weak and the needy, including slaves. However, there are also significant differences. The Hebrew texts are monotheistic, and the motive for behavior is obedience to the Lord who freed them from Egyptian bondage and established a covenant relationship with them.

According to Leviticus there were two kinds of slaves in ancient Israel: indentured Hebrews (25:39-43), and Gentile (*"goyim"*) slaves (25:44-46). There were provisions for freeing the former; the latter were considered slaves for life.

Consider the plight of a small Israelite farmer who fell into debt and became more and more dependent on his creditor. As he slipped deeper and deeper into debt he mortgaged his children and then his land. Finally, after becoming totally bankrupt he sold himself to his creditor. This was drastic action!

However, there were two restrictions on the creditor that protected the bonded servant. As an Israelite, the servant was "kin" and not a *"goy."* The owner could not rob him of his dignity. The fellow Israelite could not be sold on an open market. The owner should not rule over him "with harshness" (Leviticus 25:43). The fear of God put limits on abuse and terror. The socially and economically inferior person stood in the same covenant relationship to the Lord as the powerful party. Secondly, the indentured party was to be released in the jubilee year (Leviticus 25:40, 41). The maximum time of hired service for an Israelite would be fifty years. However, older texts in Exodus 21:1-6 and Deuteronomy 15:12-18 provided for release after six years of obligatory service. The confusion arises from separate sources of the texts.

These restrictions did not apply to non-Israelite slaves (Leviticus 25:44-46). As property, these *"goyim"* were slaves for life. They could be bought from other Gentiles and presumably sold at the owner's discretion. These verses are puzzling when compared with Leviticus 19:33-34:

> When an alien resides with you in your land, you shall not oppress the alien. The alien who resides with you shall be to you as the citizen among you; you shall love the alien as yourself; for you were aliens in the land of Egypt: I am the Lord your God.

Even when it is granted that there was one law for the alien and one for the Israelite citizen (cf. Leviticus 24:22 and Exodus 12:49), there is no clear answer to the contradiction between Leviticus 25:44-46 and 19:33-34. One commentator suggests that the former verses might have been a concession to large property holders who owned slaves. Citing the example of the Puritans, who initially justified slavery from the Old Testament, Gerstenberger writes: "Leviticus 25:44-46, as the only express allowance to keep slaves in the entire Bible, has had disasterous consequences."[10]

There were occasions when an Israelite became indentured to a Gentile (25:47). Then he could be redeemed by a relative upon payment of the purchase price. The order of kinship for redemption was stated in a descending line: brother, uncle, cousin, other family members (25:48-49). Or as a hired worker with a meager wage, he might save enough over a period of time to redeem himself. The amount of the purchase price was carefully calculated, based on a proportion of the price for service to the next jubilee year (25:50-52). The Israelite was to refund that part of the price for which he had not served. While the man was indentured the fellow Israelites had the responsibility "to watch" that the Gentile owner did not abuse him. If all efforts to free him failed, then he must serve until released in the jubilee year. It is interesting that this was a personal release with no reference to land. The foreigner had no right to take the inheritance of an Israelite under any circumstances.

Leviticus 25 concludes with a solemn claim to the Lord's ownership of the Israelites. Having freed them from Egyptian bondage, they are his people and must serve no other gods.

During the siege of Jerusalem in 587 B.C. by the Babylonians, King Zedekiah made a proclamation that freed all Hebrew slaves. His act was in accordance with the covenant provisions that Hebrew slaves should be released after six years of service (Exodus 21:2; Deuteronomy 15:12). The king's decree was implemented. But when the siege was lifted the aristocrats put the newly liberated slaves back into subjection. This enraged the prophet Jeremiah; the leaders had profaned the name of the Lord. "Therefore, thus says the Lord: you have not obeyed me by granting a release to your neighbors and friends; I am going to grant a release to you, says the Lord—a release to the sword, to pestilence, and to famine" (Jeremiah 34:17). The prophet plays on the word "release" with grim irony. There will be a release, but it will not be to freedom, but to the horrors of war, disease, and famine.

Slavery as a legal institution has finally been abolished in all countries, although it survives in practice in certain areas of the world. An important issue in our society is criminal justice and the penal system. In the United States the prison population has doubled in the last twelve years, with 1.8 million people in American jails and prisons in 1998. There were 668 inmates for every 100,000 U. S. residents in June 1998, compared with 313 inmates per 100,000 in 1985.[11] The article also notes that Minnesota is at the lowest end of the state and federal prison population, with 117 prisoners for every 100,000 population. One reason is Minnesota's policy to reserve prison stays for its most serious offenders.

What changes in policy and practice might slow or even reverse the national trend to build more prisons and incarcerate more people? One penitentiary warden said his responsibility was to feed and house the prisoners and protect the public; rehabilitation was not in his vocabulary. This is quite amazing! What changes for the better can society expect from released prisoners with such a policy?

What provision is made for psychological and spiritual counselling? What programs exist for learning skills and money management? What reorientation programs exist for reentry into public life?

Over 70% of American prisoners are non-violent offenders who are often incarcerated with hardened criminals. Prisons become schools for crime rather than institutions with the goal of rehabilitation. This is inhumane to prisoners and counterproductive to society. Might there be better ways to deal with many of these persons? In practice this would combine education and counselling with more use of electonic monitoring, house arrest, and work release programs. Could the American criminal justice system and penal institutions give more consideration and priority to these alternatives in the coming Year of Jubilee and in the future?

FORGIVING DEBTS—"JUBILEE 2000"

There is anticipation and excitement as the second millennium closes and the third millennium dawns. Some Christians, notably certain dispensationalists, are predicting that the rapture and the return of Christ is imminent. Jack Van Impe, for example, believes that Christ will return in the next ten years. Periodicals issue special editions on the subject. The secular world also gets into the action, out of necessity getting ready for Y2K. But there is also jostling by companies, like Coca-Cola, to capture advertising opportunities. Hotels and restaurants expect capacity crowds to celebrate the last night of 1999.

But there will be no celebration for many of the world's citizens. In the year 2000 over 1.5 billion people will continue in poverty and 40 percent of children in the developing world will be malnourished. Debt is one of the causes of this deepening poverty. Ordinary working people living in the 40 to 45 poorest nations, usually referred to as the Third World, had no say in incurring these debts and have no way out from this crushing burden.

Consider additional facts and factors of this international problem. For a billion people, development is now being thrown into reverse. After several decades of economic advance, many third world countries are sliding back into poverty. In the world's 37 poorest countries, spending per person has gone down 50 percent on health care and 25 percent on education. Africa now spends four times more on interest on its loans than on health care. Over 500,000 children die each year because of cutbacks to health services. Former president of Tanzania Julius Nyerere asks, "Must we starve our children to pay our debt?" According to Jubilee 2000/USA some 30 percent of the children of sub-Sahara Africa are undernourished, and malnutrition accounts for half of all the deaths of preschool children.

These conditions contribute to social and ecological problems. The economic and social instability from its debt played a major role in the collapse of Rwanda. In some countries, debt fuels the drug trade as poor farmers turn to growing high value cash crops like opium and cocaine. In other areas, rainforests are being destroyed and the land cleared; the timber and beef are sold in foreign currency to pay back debts.

"Jubilee 2000" is a worldwide campaign launched to address the enormous debt problem. It is inspired by Leviticus 25 and its jubilee year when slaves are freed and debts are cancelled. Personnel from 69 countries are involved in "Jubilee 2000." It is supported by dozens of Protestant, Roman Catholic, and ecumenical organizations, including Church World Services, and Bread for the World. In November 1997 Pope John Paul II issued a forceful statement asking multilateral institutions to forgive the foreign debt of developing nations. He said that "Christians will have to raise their voices on behalf of the poor of all the world. The Jubilee is an appropriate time to give thought to reducing substantially, or cancelling, the debt which seriously threatens many nations."[12]

One of the most zealous sponsors of "Jubilee 2000" is Bread for the World (BFW), a non-partisan Christian citizens' movement that is dedicated to ending poverty. BFW's theme is "Proclaim Jubilee: Break the Chain of Debt." Through literature and letter writing BFW endeavors to inform and influence elected officials on a variety of issues, particularly the debt of financially strapped countries. They have a video portraying the struggle of a family in Tanzania makes the story poignant and personal.[13] Let Tanzania's debt and this family's situation illustrate the plight of millions.

In the introductory part of the video, Mr. Steves gives a brief discussion of Tanzania's current debt problem. Tanzania became independent from Great Britain in 1964. It carries the weight of 30 years of accumulated debt owed to wealthy countries. Some of the borrowed money was used for helpful projects, but other programs have been failures. Only one-tenth of the loans have been used to develop agricultural projects. Tanzania now owes seven billion dollars to the United States and other developed countries; this is nearly four-fifths of its national budget. Current debt payments fall far short of meeting the annual payment of principle and interest. Basic needs for roads, health care, and education are neglected.

The situation of the Masarieki family is presented in the video. Like 80 percent of Tanzanians, Samweli and Rebecca Masarieki make their living in agriculture. They raise several crops for food, but their only cash crop is raw coffee beans. These sell for a dollar a pound and in a good year they can sell 1800 pounds. A good harvest will feed them and their children, but with drought there is the real threat of hunger. However, the national debt is another problem, and a chronic one even when the weather is favorable. Their coffee crop yields have fallen, and this is partly due to the national debt. Tanzania's debt payments and a devalued currency have reduced the subsidy for imported fertilizers and insecticides. Without the subsidy these products are too expensive for the Masarieki family. Worms on the coffee plants must be picked off by hand. Production is drastically lowered.

The Masarieki children go to a primary school with 60 children in one room. Parents pay fees even in primary schools and the fees have been increased due to the national debt. The fees have also increased in secondary schools and the Masariekis will be unable to send their children unless conditions change. In Tanzania only one child in 20 attends a secondary school. Millions of Tanzanian children are working instead of studying in school. For every dollar spent on debt payment, only a quarter is spent on health care. The health care system of Tanzania is limping along; people must pay for medicines or go without. Malaria, yellow fever, and cholera may go untreated. Life expectancy is 50 years; one child in six dies before his/her fifth birthday.

Another African country, Uganda, has a 3.5 billion dollar foreign debt and is one of the most severely indebted countries in the world. The government spends ten times more repaying foreign debt than it does for primary health care. Doctors and health care workers are some of the lowest paid professionals in Uganda, and many go to other countries for better pay. About 60 percent of the people live in poverty. Much of Uganda's debt was incurred under past oppressive regimes, especially that of Idi Amin. Foes of this tyrant would refer to him, not inappropriately, as "Idiot Amin." Uganda owes much of its debt to creditors such as the World Bank and the International Monetary Fund. Despite its hardships, under present leadership it has been a model debtor in repaying creditors. However, lower coffee prices in the last ten years have put Uganda deeper and deeper into the debt trap. Bread for the World urges that Uganda receive the maximum amount of debt relief as soon as possible, provided it invests the savings in basic health and education services.[14]

Nicaragua in Central America is suffering the worst economic crisis in its history. Every man, woman, and child owes about $3,000 to foreign creditors, making it the most indebted country per capita in the world. The crisis began with the global recession in the early 1980s when prices for its exports declined sharply. The U. S. sponsored war and an economic boycott against the left-leaning Sandanista government in the 1980s caused Nicaragua to borrow heavily from Eastern bloc countries to finance the war and prop up its economy. With Violeta Charmorro's presidential victory in 1990 the United States ended its boycott. Since then deregulation of the economy and reduced public services have been particularly bad for poor people. In 1991 Nicaragua spent less than $17 per person for health care, compared with $58 in 1988; per capita spending on education dropped from $42 in 1984 to $13 in 1993. There has been some debt relief.

In 1990, in support of the new Charmorro government, the United States forgave almost 90 percent of the debt. In 1996, after six years of negotiation, Russia made a significant reduction of Nicaragua's debt. Bread for the World urges U. S. development aid as well as further debt relief, conditioned on Nicaragua's commitment to poverty reduction.[15]

The cancelling of foreign debts is hardly a novel idea. In 1991 the United States forgave Egypt's debt of several billion dollars in exchange for that country's support of the Gulf War. Nor is it, in the final analysis, an act of charity. In 1993 rich nations took back three dollars in debt payments for every dollar they gave in aid.

Accountability is built into debt relief. For example, current bills in Congress would require each country to establish a Human Development Fund. Its savings would be used to reduce the number of persons living in poverty, expand basic social services to the poorest members of society, and prevent the degradation of the environment. Countries that support international terrorism and drug trafficking and have gross violations of human rights would be excluded from debt relief.

The potential benefits of debt relief are significant. Foremost is saving millions of children from disease and hunger, especially in Africa. It would also have a positive effect on the environment because debt induced poverty causes exploitation of natural resources. Debt creates social unrest and war, so debt relief should increase global security. And it would increase exports from rich countries to poorer nations, stimulating employment and protecting jobs in countries like Canada and the United States.

The basic motivation for Christians in "Jubilee 2000" comes from Leviticus 25 and Jesus' ministry and proclamation of "good news to the poor" (Luke 4:16 ff.). The poor who are strapped with a large debt have had basic human services reduced while there still isn't enough money to pay the debt. The vicious circle must be cut! Jubilee calls for renewal through debt relief that would give millions of poor and hungry families a new beginning and hope for the future.

JESUS AND JUBILEE

There is no text more important for understanding Luke's writing than the Nazareth synagogue pericope. While Mark (6:1-6) has a Nazareth visit that also ended in rejection, the substance of Luke's account with the readings from Isaiah is unique to him. It is a programmatic section in the third Gospel. The narrative is dramatic and descriptive with themes that summarize Jesus' ministry. Luke is providing us with glasses through which we should read the rest of the story.

THE JUBILEE AND JESUS

In a superb prologue, written in classical Greek, Luke sets forth his credentials and purpose for writing his gospel (Luke 1:1-4). Though he was not an eyewitness of Jesus' ministry, Luke trusted the oral tradition of those who had been with Jesus. His motivation for writing was "to set down an orderly account of the events that have been fulfilled among us" (1:1). He then lists his own credentials as a writer and historian; they are "completeness" (*anothen*), "thoroughness" (*pasin*), "accuracy" (*akribos*), and a claim to an "orderly" (*kathexas*) narrative. His purpose for writing is to give the catechumen Theophilus the "truth" (*asphaleia*) concerning the things in which he had been instructed.

Luke's credentials are evident in the gospel narrative. Luke does not begin with Jesus' ministry, as Mark did, nor with Jesus' genealogy and birth, as Matthew did. He begins with the announcement to Zechariah of the birth of John the Baptist, the forerunner to Jesus. He ends his two-volume work, considering Luke-Acts as a continuous narrative, with Paul the apostle in Rome. This is "completeness" and "thoroughness." Luke's claim to "accuracy" states his intention to be careful in his narrative so that Theophilus would have the truth and could build his life on it. Luke's claim to an "orderly" account does not necessarily mean chronological order of events, but order of signficance. In his narrative, Luke is bearing "witness" to the events of salvation history. For example, the temptations in Luke 4:1-13 are in an ascending order of significance compared with Matthew. Jesus goes to Nazareth and later to Capernaum, which is in reverse order from both Mark and Matthew.

The prior visit to Jesus' hometown of Nazareth in Luke 4:16-30 is of special significance. Luke makes this event a prelude to and a thematic section of Jesus' Galilean ministry (4:14—9:50).

Filled with the power of the Holy Spirit from his baptism (3:21-22), and having successfully resisted the devil's temptations (4:1-13), Jesus returned to Galilee where his early synagogue teaching won universal praise (4:14-15). The Nazareth synagogue narrative is quite a different story (4:16-30).

Having returned to his hometown of Nazareth, Jesus went to the synagogue on the sabbath day, as was his custom. The narrative offers interesting insights into synagogue worship at the time of Jesus. There was a democratic spirit so it was not unusual for a visitor to share in the service. Jesus stood up to read. Having received the scroll *he found* the text to read. It was from the prophet Isaiah. Was it the appointed lesson for that day or did Jesus choose it? Luke does not tell us. For Jesus, Isaiah's prophetic words established the framework for his message. The reading was also one of the most familiar and treasured texts of promise in Israel's worship, like the words in Handel's "Messiah" are for us.

> The Spirit of the Lord is upon me, because he has anointed me to bring good news to the poor. He has sent me to proclaim release to the captives and recovery of sight to the blind, to let the oppressed go free, to proclaim the year of the Lord's favor (Luke 4:18-19).

With its liberation theme, Isaiah is the bridge between the exodus and the gospels. Closing the book, Jesus handed it back to the synagogue attendant, and sat down. The people sat there in rapt silence, gazing intently at Jesus. After a pause, he broke the silence:

> Today this scripture has been fulfilled in your hearing" (Luke 4:21).

This one sentence sums up his sermon. Jesus leaves no middle ground—"everything written about me in the law of Moses, the prophets, and the psalms must be fulfilled" (Luke 24:44). The prophecy and the proclaimer now confronted those who saw and heard him. What claims was Jesus making?

At Jesus' baptism Luke states that the Holy Spirit descended upon Jesus in bodily form like a dove and the voice from heaven declared him to be God's beloved Son (3:21-22; cf. Mark 1:9-11 and Matthew 3:13-17). Full of the Holy Spirit, he was led by the Spirit in the wilderness for 40 days while tempted by the devil (4:1-13).

Jesus returned in the power of the Spirit to Galilee, teaching in the synagogues (4:14-15).

Now in his inaugural sermon at Nazareth, Jesus utters the astounding words that he has been anointed by God's Spirit to proclaim good news to the poor. As the anointed one, he is endowed with divine kingship and power (God's "Moshiach" or Messiah). Jesus is announcing that God's reign on earth is now beginning with his ministry and mission. The Spirit of the Lord has anointed Jesus to announce the good news and put it into effect in words and actions.

This is good news of deliverance to the poor, the oppressed, the captives, and the disabled. Its climax is Jesus' proclamation of "the year of the Lord's favor," a time of restitution and restoration when God's rule of justice will be revealed in Israel. This is the "Gospel of the Jubilee."

The lesson that Jesus read was from Isaiah 61:1-2 and 58:6. Luke's quotation is from the Greek Septuagint translation of the Hebrew Bible. This great message was originally delivered by the sixth century prophet to the exiles returning from the Babylonian captivity. It was a political jubilee that Second Isaiah proclaimed, when the captives and prisoners should be free and the Lord would give them a garland instead of ashes and the oil of gladness instead of mourning (Isaiah 61:3). God had done a "new thing," a second exodus, in the return of the captives from Babylon to Palestine (Isaiah 43:18-19). Six hundred years later, Jesus applied the message directly to himself. He took the Isaiah scriptures, woven out of the Babylonian exile, wrapped it around himself and gave it a wider meaning. This Isaiah prophecy summarized his mission, a jubilee proclamation of release and redemption.

The phrase "to let the oppressed go free" ("to set at liberty those who are oppressed," RSV) is from Isaiah 58:6. This is a powerful expression that declares "release" to those who have been crushed. The Greek word for release is "*aphesis,*" which is frequently used in the Septuagint text of Leviticus 25 to express the deliverance made in the jubilee year. It is highly unlikely that Jesus would have switched from Isaiah 61 to Isaiah 58 and back again. Instead he joins the two in his reading and exposition. With the phrase from Isaiah 58:6 he makes the message of release the more powerful, and this emphasis reached its climax in the last line of the text: "to proclaim the year of the Lord's favor."

The initial reaction of the synagogue worshipers was admiration and wonder. "Is not this Joseph's son?" (4:22) They were astonished that a hometown boy from the village of Nazareth could speak so well (cf. John 1:46). But their attitude soon turned to disgust that one of their own could make such claims. To paraphrase: "He's too big for his britches!" Now show us your authority by doing miracles like you did in neighboring Capernaum! Jesus counters the challenge with a parable (Luke 4:23) that exposes their petty jealousy and unbelief. Later in his ministry Jesus would hear similar demands for signs from Pharisees and other antagonists. A prophet is without honor in his own country!

Jesus presses the issue with stories from the Hebrew scriptures that challenge their prejudice and limited horizons. The prophets Elijah and Elisha were examples of God's judgment to his unbelieving people. Elijah was sent in a time of famine to minister to a pagan widow of Zarephath (I Kings 17); Elisha persuaded the leprous heathen soldier Naaman from Syria to bathe in the Jordan waters and be healed (II Kings 5). The outcasts and even the Gentiles received the prophets and the blessing of God before the elect of Israel!

This was outrageous news to the citizens of Nazareth. They assumed that God's messenger would bring good news of liberation to Israel and judgment upon the Gentiles. Yet Jesus was announcing just the opposite; Israel was facing judgment and Gentiles were being offered salvation. Nazareth was not an isolated example; their anger would have been shared in synagogues throughout Israel.

The synagogue narrative ends tragically. In their rage the worshippers drove Jesus out of the village to the edge of a cliff, intending to execute him. They had reached a verdict about him but also rendered one about themselves. But Jesus, who is more than a match for human and superhuman forces (Luke 4:1-13), walked through their midst and went on his way.

The synagogue narrative is programmatic for Jesus' ministry in Galilee (Luke 4:14-9:50), the long journey to Jerusalem (9:51-19-48), and the last days in Jerusalem (chapters 20-24). The Galilean ministry opened with rejection in Nazareth (4:16-30); the journey to Jerusalem likewise began with a rejection (9:51-56). The themes of promise and fulfilment, rejection and suffering, are developed in the rising action of Luke's gospel, climaxing in the cross and resurrection.

Jesus Messiah stands in the grand tradition of the Old Testament prophets. Like them, he and John the Baptist spoke words of judgment to Israel as well as to the nations. This sets them apart from contemporary Jewish teachers who exempted elect Israel from judgment. And the apocalyptists at Qumran, while condemning the apostate Israelites from whom they had separated as well as all Gentiles, believed that they alone would survive the final war (cf. *The War of the Sons of Light with the Sons of Darkness* in the Dead Seas Scrolls literature). But Jesus even stands apart from John in proclaiming forgiveness and hope. When John in prison had doubts about Jesus as Messiah he sent two disciples with the question: "Are you he who is to come, or shall we look for another?" Jesus' marvelous answer points to the evidence: "Go and tell John what you have seen and heard: the blind receive their sight, and the lame walk, lepers are cleansed, and the deaf hear, the dead are raised up, the poor have good news preached to them" (RSV, Luke 7:18-23=Matthew 11:1-6, "Q"). The Messianic age is here, coupled with the jubilee.

While the Nazareth synagogue narrative is the jubilee pericope "par excellence" in the New Testament, there are other passages with the jubilee theme. I mention two that are particularly significant. The "Our Father" prayer (Luke 11:2-4=Matthew 6:9-13, "Q") that Jesus taught the disciples contains the jubilee petition of forgiveness (*"aphesis"*). The petition in Matthew is even more explicit than the one in Luke: "And forgive us our debts, as we also have forgiven our debtors" (Matthew 6:12). The parable of the unforgiving servant (Matthew 18:23-35) is Jesus' response to Peter's question about how often he should forgive one who had sinned against him. Forgiveness is beyond calculation!

The "Year of Jubilee," named for the "shofar" that ushered it in, was that divine provision for social and economic justice in agrarian Israel. It provided rest for land and people and animals, a periodic redistribution of capital, and a safeguard for family inheritance and livelihood. Affirming this program of renewal, Jesus follows in the steps of the priest who, with the "shofar" horn, ushered in "the year of the Lord's favor." He finds in the jubilee a model of the eschatological Messianic year, a year that will bring release and forgiveness of sins to people of all nations and usher in an era of liberty and gladness.[1] With fulfilment of the vision of Isaiah, Jesus proclaims himself as the world's evangelist, healer, liberator, and Savior.

ENDNOTES

Chapter 1

1. Schaff, Philip, *History of the Christian Church. Volume IV.* Grand Rapids: Eerdmans, 1910. 280.
2. Schaff, 206-07.
3. Schaff, 296.
4. "Sect members meet violent end." *Christian Century* 111,19 October 1994. 944f.
5. *The Washington Times Jerusalem.* 11 January 1999.

Chapter 2

1. Clouse, Robert G. (ed. and introd.), *The Meaning of the Millenium: Four Views.* Downers Grove, IL: Intervarsity Press, 1977. "Amillennialism," Anthony A. Hoekema, 155.
2. Hoekema, 156.
3. Clouse, 11
4. Boettner, Loraine, op. cit. "Postmillennialism."
5. Boettner, 118.
5. Boettner, 138.
6. Ladd, George Eldon, in response to Boettner, 143.

Chapter 3

1. Bowman, John Wick. "II. Dispensationalism." *Interpretation. A Journal of Bible and Theology.* 10 (January 1956): 173-178.
2. Kittel, Gerhard (ed.), *Theological Dictionary of the New Testament. Volume I,* trans. and ed. Geoffrey Bromiley. Grand Rapids: William B. Eerdmans, 1964. 380-81. Written records of this custom can also be dated to John Chrysostom, AD 347-407, *The Ascension of Our Lord* and *Homilies on Thessalonians,* Homily 8.
3. Allis, Oswald T., quotation from L. S. Chafer, *Prophecy and the Church.* Philadelphia: The Presbyterian and Reformed Publishing Company, 1945. 20-21.

4. Boyer, Paul, *When Time Shall Be No More.* Cambridge: Harvard University Press, 1992. 182.

5. Boyer, 183.

6. Boyer, 183-84.

7. Boyer, 186.

8. "Balfour Declaration." *Encyclopedia Americana.* 1990 ed. See also Paul Boyer, *When Time Shall Be No More.* 101-02, 186, 190, 200, 294.

9. Weber, Timothy P., "How Evangelicals Became Israel's Best Friend," *Christianity Today"* 42, 5 October 1998. 45. The article is pages 39-49.

10. Lindsey, Hal, *The Late Great Planet Earth.* Grand Rapids: Zondervan, 1970. Bantam, 1973.

11. Marsden, George M., *Fundamentalism and American Culture.* New York: Oxford University Press, 1980. 55.

12. Marsden, 55.

13. Charlesworth, James H. (ed.), *The Old Testament Pseudepigrapha, Volume I. Apocalyptic Literature and Testaments.* Garden City: Doubleday, 1983. There are several collections of Qumran literature; the most recent is edited by Geza Vermes, *The Complete Dead Sea Scrolls in English.* New York: Penguin Press, 1997.

14. Farrer, Austin, *A Rebirth of Images: The Making of John's Apocalypse.* Boston: Beacon Press, 1949, 1963. 19-20.

Chapter 4

1. Rasmussen, Larry, *Earth Community, Earth Ethics.* Maryknoll: Orbis Books, 1996. 232.

2. Rasmussen, 230-36.

3. Brueggemann, Walter, *Genesis: A Bible Commentary for Teaching and Preaching.* Atlanta: John Knox Press, 1982. 35-36.

4. Schumacher, E. F., *Small is Beautiful: Economics as if People Mattered.* New York: Harper & Row, 1973. 95-109. Also Walter Brueggemann, *The Land.* Philadelphia: Fortress Press, 1977.

5. Leopold, Aldo, *A Sand County Almanac.* New York: Ballantine Books, 1949, 1966.

6. Leopold, 264-69.

7. Quoted by Al Gore in *Earth in the Balance.* Boston: Houghton Mifflin Company, 1992. 259.

8. Leopold, 262.

9. Quoted in an article by Dale Thorenson, "Heartland is losing its farm-

ers at an alarming rate." Minneapolis *Star Tribune,* 26 April 1999. A 11.

10. Gerstenberger, Erhard S., *Leviticus. A Commentary,* trans. by Douglas W. Stott. Louisville: Westminster John Knox Press, 1996. 390-91. See also Lee Griffith, *The Fall of the Prison. Biblical Perspectives on Prison Abolition,* Grand Rapids: Eerdmans 1993; and Howard Zehr, *Changing Lenses.* Scottsdale, PA: Herald Press, 1990.

11. Minneapolis *Star Tribune.* 15 March 1999. A 1.

12. *Jubilee 2000/USA* (pamphlet).

13. Video: *Proclaim Jubilee. Break the Chains of Debt.* Narrated by Rick Steves. A Raisz-Sheridan Production for Bread for the World. 1999.

14. *Debt Burdens Threaten Uganda Success* by Kathy Selvaggio and Amy Jersild. Bread for the World, Silver Spring, MD. (pamphlet).

15. *Debt Devours Poor People in Nicaragua* by Kathy Selvaggio and Amy Jersild. Bread for the World, Silver Spring, MD. (pamphlet).

Chapter 5

1. Video: *Jesus and Jubilee: A Biblical Study on Economic Justice* Parts I and II. Narrated by Sarah Henrich. The Peace with Justice Committee of the Minneapolis and St. Paul, Minnesota Area Synods, ELCA, with assistance from Tamela Walhof, Regional Coordinator, Bread for the World, Minneapolis, Minnesota.